Stories of Uncle Adrian
A Guide to Mastery in Your Life

Stories of Uncle Adrian
A Guide to Mastery in Your Life

Zan Monroe

To my children,
Louisa and Cameron

Published by:
The Monroe Company, Inc.
P. O. Box 58241
Fayetteville, NC 28305
www.StoriesofUncleAdrian.com

First Edition
Printed and bound in the United States of America by Morris Publishing
www.morrispublishing.com • 800-650-7888
12345678910

Table of Contents

Part Four - The Value of Joy

Part Five - Mastery in Business

Part 6 - Mastering Your Finances

Part 7 - Becoming Master of Your Own Life

INTRODUCTION

When my father died four days before my eleventh birthday, I became the man of the family, thinking I had to look after my mother and three older sisters. A great deal of my life has been spent searching for adult role models. I found that television had John Wayne and James Arness on Gunsmoke. Ian Fleming's James Bond was a good hero to read about. Harold Lovick, my father's best friend, taught me about hunting and fishing but my greatest adult role models were my mother and her brothers and sisters, the Williams family.

My fondest memories as a child were those times when my mother and her brothers and sisters would gather around that big lazy-susan table in our kitchen, talking. They would discuss life, politics, or business, and then one of them would tell a story that made them all howl with laughter.

Uncle Don and Uncle Adrian told most of the stories. Uncle Don built houses. Uncle Adrian was a businessman who was a great after-dinner speaker. He spoke at the Lions Club or other meetings to entertain with his stories and teach lessons about business and life. He was a self-made millionaire. He liked to say that he had a story for every occasion. Anyone who knew Uncle Adrian had a favorite Uncle Adrian story.

I have used Uncle Adrian's lessons to become successful, but I have never forgotten his stories. Over the years, I have become a professional speaker and teacher, inspiring and educating thousands of people each year. As I developed my presentations about mastery in life, I found myself telling the stories that I had heard from my Uncle Adrian, Uncle Don, and the rest of the Williams family.

Storytelling has always been an effective and enjoyable way for people to communicate, and Uncle Adrian's stories have taught many lessons over the years about mastery in business and in life. Not all of the stories contained in this book are Uncle Adrian's; in fact, most of the stories that Uncle Adrian told were not originally his anyway. He simply collected stories wherever he went, remembered them, attached lessons to them, and passed them on — making the world a better place.

Before you begin this book, you should look at your present mental state and attitude. Are you in a learning mood? Are there are areas of your life that need improvement? Are you in a receptive frame of mind? Have you accepted the possibility that this book has something valuable to share with you and that you need to receive it?

Mastery in life is difficult, but if you are willing to do the work of self-examination and to bear the pain of changing yourself, then all the success in the world is yours to have. As my Uncle Adrian always said, "If it was easy, everyone would do it."

You are not controlled by your past. No matter what your life is like right now you can change it simply by changing your mind. Regardless of the kind of past relationships you have had, you are not controlled by a broken heart. Wherever you are, that is where you must begin. As my mother always said, "No matter where you are, well, there you are." It is not where you are but what is in you that counts. Joy is not found in people, places, or things. Joy is within you through your daily adventure with life. Never, ever, ever give up on your search for personal mastery. Remember that the last human freedoms are to choose your own attitude in any given set of circumstances and to choose your own way.

I've divided the Stories of Uncle Adrian into six areas of mastery. They are your physical body, your spiritual and educational growth, your relationship with yourself and others, your ability to experience joy, your business or occupation and your finances. If you work toward mastery in each of these areas *every day* you will be the master of your own life

Stewart Emery defines mastery as requiring "that we constantly produce results beyond and out of the ordinary. Mastery is a product of consistently going beyond our limits.....If you're willing to commit yourself to excellence, to surround yourself with things that represent this excellence, your life will change."

My hope is that these stories and the lessons they teach will become a guide to mastery in your business and in your life. Use these stores as your own. I do not own them. I am just a storyteller, telling stories to inspire and educate. Maybe there are some stories and lessons here that you can pass on to your friends or family. My goal is to inspire and educate one million people by January 1, 2010. Help me reach that goal by sharing a story and a lesson with someone you love today.

PART ONE

Physical Mastery

Uncle Adrian was a drill sergeant during World War II

"To make ends meet, You have to get off of one of them."
Uncle Adrian

If Your Food Could Talk:
A Parrot for Christmas

If your food could talk, what would it say? Would it tell you that it was good or bad for you? Well, if your food could talk, maybe it would tell you what to eat…and then again maybe you would not listen.

Are you listening to what you are eating, or are you just eating whatever is in front of you? Take the time necessary to examine your diet. Begin to evaluate the things you eat so that you can determine whether they are good for you. Here are some guidelines for a healthy diet.

You must eat in order to have a lean, healthy body. One of the worst things you can do to your body is to starve it. Not eating sets off alarms in your body that tell it to save fat, just in case you have to go without food for an extended period of time. As long as you are getting food on a constant basis your body will believe that it does not need to store fat.

You should consume six nutritious meals a day. Thousands of years ago we were hunter-gatherers, and we grazed for food all day long. You should eat six small meals every day instead of three large ones. If you get hungry, eat. Just do not eat very much. Eat enough to satisfy yourself for the next couple of hours, and at the end of that time, eat again.

*Each meal should contain high-quality protein such as fish or chicken, carbohydrates in the form of potatoes, whole-grain rice and all the vegetables you want.*Each portion of food should be about the size of your fist or the palm of your hand.

Studies show that you need vitamins because you are not eating food that has just been picked out of the garden. The vegetables and fruits that you see in the grocery store begin to lose vitamins and minerals from the moment they are harvested. Cooking removes more of the valuable vitamins and minerals from your food. Here is a suggested daily vitamin regimen: a good multi-vitamin, plus Vitamin C, Vitamin E, B-Complex, and Glutamine.

If you need to find out more about vitamins, there is a health food store in your area. Stop in tomorrow and talk with the expert behind the counter. What if your body needed a vitamin that was not there? Would you spend a few pennies a day to provide your body with the essential nutrients it requires?

Your body needs ten cups of water a day. The average person does not drink enough water. If you wait until you feel thirsty to drink water, you have waited too long. Caffeinated drinks take additional water from your body to process the caffeine — so if you drink only soft drinks rather than water, you will be in a constant state of dehydration. Your body is seventy-five percent water, and the loss of just one pint can cause irritability, a loss of concentration, and diminished physical performance. Drinking water when you are tired will give you more energy.

Certain foods are fat-burning foods. If you want a lean body, eat more high-fiber vegetables, deep-water fish, egg whites, berries and cook with extra-virgin olive oils.

Uncle Adrian used to tell a story about a family who got a parrot for Christmas. Their son took a job with an oil company, and his employer transferred him to South America. He sent word that he would not be coming home for Christmas.

Around the first of December his parents received a large, colorful parrot in the mail with a note that said, "Merry Christmas, Mom and Dad. Everyone here loves these birds, so I thought you would like to have one for Christmas. Your loving son, John."

His parents kept the bird in a cage and had to listen to it screech and yell until Christmas. After the New Year, their son called and asked how they liked the bird. Their response was that the bird was delicious!

"You ate it?" John cried. "That bird was very valuable. He would have cost over a thousand dollars in the United States and that bird could talk."

"Well," said his mother "he should have said something."

If your food could talk, would you listen? Begin to focus on what you are eating every day, and you will begin the journey toward becoming master of your physical body.

Do You Live to Eat or Eat to Live? Shall We Gather at the River?

Are you on a diet today? Certainly you are. Everyone is on a diet. It is just that some people pay attention to what they eat, while others are on the "see food diet." You know, eating all the food they "see."

Food is the most powerful drug you will ever put into your body, and you do that three to six times a day. Food affects every part of your life. It can change your mood, affect your thinking, and cause you to become more or less aware of your surroundings.

Crash diets to lose weight do not work, because you cannot create a short-term solution to a long-term issue. You cannot stop eating any more than you can stop breathing. A three-day diet is just a three-day solution, and it will not work on a long-term basis. You must take control of your eating habits for the rest of your life.

You must learn how to feed your body what it needs to function properly. Our diet over the last 10,000 years has consisted mostly of fruits, vegetables, nuts, grains, fish, and meats. In the past fifty years or so, we have introduced processed foods into the equation. We eat breads, crackers, and cookies consisting mostly of refined sugar. Our fast food is made mostly with hydrogenated oils. We consume frozen, concentrated, prepackaged, prepared, and processed foods that resemble real foods but are not real at all.

You should also limit your use of caffeine, sugar and alcohol. Caffeine is the drug of choice for our world today. We consume great quantities of it everyday in coffee, tea and caffeinated drinks. Sugar is in almost all processed foods. It is added as a preservative and to make everything taste better. Alcohol is touted by some as a health benefit but that is only in small quantities.

Uncle Adrian never consumed alcohol. However he loved to tell the story about a temperance sermon he heard long ago entitled "Shall We Gather at the River?"

One Sunday at church the minister was preaching on the sin of drinking. With great emphasis he said, "If I had all the beer in the world, I would pour it into the river."

With his voice rising, he said, "And if I had all the wine in the world, I would pour it into the river."

Then, shaking his fist in the air, he yelled, "And if I had all the whiskey in the world, I would pour it into the river."

Finally, to the relief of the congregation, the preacher completed his sermon and sat down. Then the music minister stood up very cautiously and announced, with a smile, nearly laughing — "For our closing song, let us sing hymn number 365, 'Shall We Gather at the River?'"

Take a moment to consider your diet. What are you eating and drinking? How much sugar, caffeine and alcohol do you consume every day? When you are master of what you put into your body, you will become master of your life. And if you are going to drink alcohol, be sure to gather at the river when you do.

Exercise Makes You Feel Good: Running Across the United States

We all know that exercise makes us feel good, but it is easy to go day after day without exercising. Our bodies build up toxins from smoke, food additives and other unnatural and dangerous things. If you get out there and play, run and sweat, your body will cleanse itself of these toxins. You pump oxygen into your brain when you exercise, and as a result you think better. Regular exercise will definitely make you feel better. Get out in the fresh air and get some exercise, and you will be rejuvenated. It is hard to be depressed when you are physically active because your body produces endorphins when you exercise that create a wonderful feeling inside.

"Oh, but I cannot." you say. Well, you could walk for ten minutes around your neighborhood tomorrow morning. You might even see some of your neighbors. After a few days of walking, something amazing will happen to you. Your mind will embrace the fact that you could do more. Your mind will say, "Hey, if I can walk ten minutes, I could do fifteen minutes — and then twenty."

After a few months you could be exercising for as much as an hour a day, which is what it takes to put you in top physical shape. And why wouldn't you want to be in top physical shape? The body you have is the only one you are going to get. You better get it into the best shape that you possibly can because it has to last you a lifetime. My mother used to say "Your body will rust out before you wear it out." Become the master of your own body and start exercising regularly.

Uncle Adrian would have loved the story of my sister Cornelia, who is a great example of what is possible if you just get off the couch and get active. Not that she was ever a couch potato, but like all of us after her college years she was no longer particularly active. Cornelia began walking for exercise, and she kept expanding her regimen a little each day until she reached an hour a day of walking.

I asked her, "Why don't you just run for a half hour instead of walking for an hour? That would save time and give you a more intense workout."

"Oh, I am not an athlete and I can't run." she replied.

"Tomorrow morning at some time during the hour that you walk, you could run from one light pole to the next, couldn't you?" I asked. Cornelia loves a challenge, and I was challenging her as only a little brother can.

She called the next day to inform me that she had run the distance of five light poles during her walk. Two weeks later she called to tell me that she had run a mile without stopping. A month later she was running two or three miles daily, then four miles, then five...

My sister, who said she could not run, has run over a thousand miles a year for the past thirteen years. She has kept a log of the miles she runs each day. She would record her miles on the calendar on her refrigerator and then add them up at the end of the month.

One day Cornelia had the great idea to run across the United States. She started plotting the miles she ran on a map. She started in Wilmington, North Carolina, where Interstate 40 begins at the Atlantic Ocean, and followed it across America until it reached the Pacific.

Every day she would run for five or six miles, in her neighborhood, recording her miles on her refrigerator at the end of the run and then transferring them each month to her map. Finally, after about eighteen months of running, she "arrived" at the Pacific Ocean. She had run across the United States — without leaving home. Oh, by the way Cornelia started running in her forties, and today she is in the best shape of her life -- in her fifties!

Stop a moment to think about how often you exercise. How often do you work out strenuously enough that your heart rate increases, your breathing gets hard, and you sweat? Your body was meant to run and play every day.

Every day you need to devote one hour to serious exercise. That is less than five percent of the time you are awake. If you exercise for at least twenty minutes with your heart rate at 180 beats per minute minus your age, then your metabolism will increase to 150% of normal for the following eighteen hours. If you are fifty years old, you should work out with a heart rate of at least 130 beats per minute (180 – 50 = 130 bpm) in order to raise your metabolism. You will burn fat at 150% your normal rate for eighteen hours following a good workout.

Start tomorrow with ten minutes of exercise, and work at it a little bit longer each day. You will be amazed at how fast your body will get into excellent physical condition. Your body is built to run and play. Give it a chance.

You cannot become master of your life until you become master of your own body. Besides, exercise makes you feel good.

Truths about Exercise: Because I Can

If you have a goal of improving your physical condition, these truths about exercise will help you.

Aerobics is any exercise that gets your heart pumping, your lungs expanding, and your blood flowing. Running, swimming, walking vigorously, riding a bike — just about anything can become an aerobic exercise if you go at it intensely enough. The key is to get your cardiovascular system working hard. Your heart is a muscle and needs exercise just as much as your arms and legs.

To transform your physique, you must train with weights. Weight training stimulates muscle growth and is the fastest way to change the shape of your body. Your body will adapt to any stress, and if you introduce stress to your muscles by lifting weights, they will respond by growing.

People of all ages can add muscle through weight-training. Don't say that you're too old to get into shape! Weight-training studies have been done on people of all ages, and they've determined that all of us benefit from serious exercise, regardless of age. When Ronald Reagan became President, he started lifting weights in the White House gym and increased two jacket sizes during his first term!

When you choose to weight-train, you should start by

weight-training three times a week, and add aerobics three times a week. Alternate your upper and lower body muscles to keep from tiring any one muscle group too much.

Muscle requires five times less space than fat, yet it also weighs more than fat. You begin to lose muscle by the age of thirty. Until you reach thirty, your body is still growing and adding muscle, but after that muscle growth will begin to decline. According to Bill Phillips in his book Body for Life, most people's body-fat content will double from ages thirty to sixty! A man will see himself add eighteen percent body fat, increasing to thirty-six percent, and a woman will go from thirty-three to forty-four percent body fat.

If you exercise, what you eat will matter even more. If you become more active, your body will need better fuel. The more active you become, the more important it will be that you eat healthy, nutritious foods to fuel your body. When you work out every day, you will also find yourself making better choices when it comes to food. Your body will tell you what it needs to be more active. You don't what to eat junk food and mess up your body after you've worked out!

Your muscles grow while you're resting and recuperating. I always thought that your muscles would grow while you were lifting weights or running. Instead, they grow while you rest! You should have a brief, intense workout and then rest so that your body can repair and strengthen your muscles.

Compare your muscles to a house that's been shaken by an earthquake. After the damage occurs, workers come in to repair everything, making the house stronger than before. Well, your body does the same thing with your muscles. When you work out, you actually damage those muscles. Then your body uses the food you eat to rebuild them even stronger than before. Each time you work out, your body goes through a similar process of rebuilding.

High-intensity effort produces the best results. The more stress you can place upon your body when you exercise, the more it will respond. Walking for twenty minutes is less beneficial for your health than twenty minutes of running. Running full speed for twenty minutes is better than jogging. And so on.

A lady I know was walking to lose some weight, but her daily walks were having no effect, so I asked her how long and how far she was walking. "Well, I walk about two miles around the lake, and it takes me an hour!" she told me. "I stop to feed the ducks, look at the sunset, and enjoy the flowers…" That is not exercise – that is a stroll!

You're much better off taking a fifteen-minute power walk than a one- hour stroll. Get going! Go for it! Be intense! If you're going to walk, *walk!* If you're running, run hard! If you're gardening or swimming or playing tennis, do it at as intensely as possible in order to receive maximum benefits.

Johnny Patterson is one of my heroes. He grew up on Middle Road in the Eastover Community near Fayetteville, North Carolina. He went to high school with my oldest sister Mary and her future husband Jerry Wade.

When Johnny played center for the Central High School basketball team, he towered over everyone else. Jerry was the point guard, and he and Johnny were best friends, making an awesome duo on and off the court.

One day not too long ago I visited Johnny Patterson in the Rehabilitation Center of Cape Fear Valley Hospital. He had been recovering from major surgery for thirteen weeks – and during all that time he had been in intensive care, on oxygen, and flat on his back! Is it any wonder that he had lost fifty pounds in the process?

Johnny's goal on the day I visited him was simply to **stand up**. In the thirteen weeks he had been in rehab he had yet to stand. Finally he stood and then he walked and eventually he even ran! He did it because he could.

I travel a lot and see many people with disabilities that do lots of things with difficulties that we take for granted. I have seen a woman with no arms traveling alone in the airport and holding her tickets with her toes. I have seen men with metal legs walking calmly toward their next flight. I have seen blind people walking with their seeing eye dogs. They do these things because they can.

What have you done today? What have you done that you have taken for granted? How much time have you spent running and playing today? What aren't you doing today that you *could* be doing just because you can?

What if you said today....

I stand up because I can.
I run because I can.
I swim because I can.
I bike because I can.
I work out every day because I can.
I lift weights because I can.
I play with my kids because I can.
I eat right and take care of my body *because I can.*

Get out there and run and *play because you can,* you could be in the hospital, flat on your back, and unable to stand.

PART TWO

Spiritual and Educational Growth

Uncle Adrian at an after dinner speech

*"Everyone has been given a talent in life.
Your job is to find out what your talent is and use
it to your fullest potential."*

Uncle Adrian

You Can Achieve Anything: The Three-Legged Chicken

You can achieve anything in your life if you do three things. First, choose a goal, and get emotionally involved in it. Second, create images in your mind so that you can clearly visualize what your life would be like *if* you achieved the goal. Third, *put into writing* what the goal means to you.

Nothing is achieved without first creating an idea. Think of the process of building a house. Someone had to get excited about the idea of building it, and then an architect had to create a vision on paper by drawing the plans for the house. Finally, the builder had to accomplish the job of building the house according to the plans.

Your mind works exactly the same way when you want to achieve a goal. First you get excited about it. Then you spend time visualizing what your world would be like if you achieved that goal. Next you map out a plan. Finally, you work until your goal is achieved.

Your mind sorts and processes information in three distinct ways. When you were a newborn, you "thought" only with emotions. You *felt* your way toward whatever you wanted to achieve. Then as you grew older, you began to *see* what you wanted. You attached pictures to the feelings you had about trying to achieve something. Finally, you were able to put *words* with the pictures and feelings to make yourself and others around you clearly understand what you wanted.

If you want to achieve a goal in life as an adult, you must follow the same process. You must have strong feelings that will drive you to achieve your goal. You must attach mental pictures to your feelings so that you can see what the goal will look like. You must write a description of how your life will benefit from your achieving the goal.

Be *careful*. If you do not clearly define your goal, you may end up achieving something that you really did not want. As Uncle Adrian used to say, "You must plan your work and work your plan." Then he would tell the story of the three-legged chicken.

One day Uncle Adrian was driving through Siler City, North Carolina, heading to Greensboro to visit the home office of Southern Life Insurance Company, his employer.

Looking out the window of his Cadillac, he noticed a chicken running along the side of the road. There was nothing unusual about seeing a chicken on the side of the road in North Carolina in the 1950's except that this chicken was running as fast as Uncle Adrian's car. His car was going thirty-five miles per hour. Uncle Adrian sped up to forty-five miles per hour, and still the chicken was keeping up with him. Then he stepped on the gas and sped the car up to fifty-five miles per hour and *still* the chicken ran effortlessly alongside him.

As Uncle Adrian and the chicken sped down the road, the woods on one side opened up into a farm, and the chicken turned down the dirt driveway and ran to the little farm house. In fact, Uncle Adrian noticed *several* chickens in the yard, all of them moving extremely fast. His curiosity got the best of him, so he slowed down, turned around, and went back to investigate.

Pulling into the driveway, Uncle Adrian noticed a farmer sitting on the porch. He got out of his car and waded through the chickens to the front steps, where Uncle Adrian bade the man a good day and said, "Sir, I know you are not going to believe me, but I think one of your chickens was running down the road as fast as my car."

"Yep" was the farmer's only answer.

"I do not think you understand," said Uncle Adrian. "I was going fifty-five miles per hour, and one of your chickens was keeping up with my car."

"Yep," the farmer replied.

"You mean to tell me that you know you have chickens that can run fifty-five miles per hour?" asked Uncle Adrian.

The farmer shifted in his rocking chair, seeming tired of the whole conversation. He had obviously had this discussion before. "My chickens can run faster than that." he said.

"Sir, please tell me about your chickens," said Uncle Adrian.

"Well, I have three daughters, and all my girls love to eat chicken. My problem is that they all like the drumstick the best. When we have fried chicken, there is always a fight because one of them does not get a drumstick. So I decided that the best way to stop the fussing was to breed a three-legged chicken. That way, everyone could get their favorite piece of chicken. The birds that you see in this yard are the result of years of working toward my goal of creating a three-legged chicken."

The farmer said all this without the least bit of satisfaction or pleasure in his voice. Uncle Adrian looked out into the front yard, and, sure enough, every chicken there had three legs. Some of them were scratching, some were pecking, but most of them were running around — very, very fast.

"Well," said Uncle Adrian, "How do they taste?"

"I do not know," said the farmer. "They are so fast that we have never been able to catch one!"

Make sure that the things you hope to achieve are clearly and specifically defined, written down, and exactly what you want. You could end up with a goal that *is not* what you want, like a bunch of three-legged chickens you cannot catch.

You need to *feel* what your future will be like when you achieve your goal. Feel what it is like to be the person who has achieved the goal. Spend time with your feelings, experiencing them fully. *Get emotionally involved with how it feels to achieve your goal.*

Create a visual future for your goal. On your refrigerator or bathroom mirror — somewhere you will look every day — put up some photos of how you envision your ideal world. Seeing those pictures every day will remind you of how things will be when you achieve your goal.

Write out all of your goals specifically, in great detail, and carry them with you so that they can remind you throughout the day of what you want to achieve. Read them aloud, and discuss them with people whom you trust to help you. There is nothing more powerful than hearing your own voice describing your future.

Carve the image of what you want into your mind, and your mind will find a way to achieve it. As my mother always said, "You can achieve anything you set your mind to."

Of course, Uncle Adrian would say, "Look out for three-legged chickens!"

Know Where You are Going: Einstein on the Train

If you know where you are going, life becomes a fantastic journey full of adventure. If you are achieving mastery in your life, you have already created a clear vision of the future you want. Before anything becomes a reality in your life, it must originate as a clear vision in your mind.

Everybody has some kind of vision of their future. Everyone takes a view of their life from the past, the present, and the future. At any point and at any age, you can see life, your life, from these three perspectives.

A person whose predominant vision of their life is focused on the past will always be looking back over the life that has already gone by. They will always be reminiscing about "the good old days" without realizing that today will be the good old days soon enough. Positive change is uncomfortable for this kind of person because it requires them to change what has always been and to create something new.

A person whose predominant vision of life deals solely with a present vision is someone who focuses on the moment at hand. They live in the present not the past. There is only the now — and now is when things get accomplished. It is true that focusing on the now is a great way to get things accomplished but if that is all you ever do, you are not anchored to a path toward your future.

A person who focuses on the future is on their way to becoming whatever they are envisioning. They are always seeking to find the best route to that future. They are concerned with where they are going and are less concerned about where they have been.

You should have three types of goals. First, you should set goals for a lifetime. These are the major things that you want to accomplish. Things like climbing mountains, running marathons, or seeing the Great Wall of China. Anything that you dream about doing should be on your lifetime-goals list.

Next, your lifetime goals should be broken down into yearly goals. Yearly goals are those steps that will eventually lead you to your lifetime goals. The question to ask is, "Of the goals on my lifetime list, which ones do I want to accomplish this year?"

Then break down each yearly goal into twelve-week segments. There's something magical about a twelve-week goal. It's long enough to influence substantial changes in your life, yet short enough to be obtainable. Each twelve-week goal should be broken down into weekly goals and daily tasks that will lead to the accomplishment of your twelve-week goals.

You should look into the six areas of mastery to see what your life's vision is for each area: physical health, educational and spiritual growth, relationships with yourself and others, joy, business and finance and then set goals in each area. Just remember that you are in a state of becoming your vision of the future — whatever that vision may be!

Once you set your goals, you should evaluate them to see whether they are realistic and detailed. Does each goal have an attainable deadline for accomplishment? Are your goals truly important to you? What are you willing to give up in order to accomplish your goals? Do all of your goals align with your future vision for your life?

Albert Einstein was once traveling from Princeton on a train when the conductor came down the aisle, punching each passenger's ticket. When he came to Einstein, the great physicist reached into his vest pocket but could not find his ticket. Then he reached into his other pocket but still could not find the ticket, so he looked into his briefcase. Nothing there. He looked at the seat beside him. Nothing.

The conductor said, "Dr. Einstein, I know who you are. We all know who you are. I'm sure you bought a ticket. Don't worry about it." Einstein nodded appreciatively, and the conductor continued down the aisle, punching tickets. When the conductor was ready to move to the next car, he happened to look back and saw Einstein down on his hands and knees, looking under his seat for the ticket.

Rushing back up the aisle, the conductor cried, "Dr. Einstein! Dr. Einstein, don't worry about your ticket! I know who you are. There's not a problem. You don't need a ticket. I'm sure you bought one!"

Einstein looked up and said, "Young man, I too know who I am. What I don't know is where I'm going!'"

Where are you going in life? Now is the time for you to get a clear vision of what you want your future to be. Then by converting your visions into reality you can form specific goals.

If you are master of your own life you will learn from the past, be focused on the present, and follow your vision to your future. Clearly define where you want to go in life and you'll never be lost. If you do not have a clear vision of your future, you are just like Einstein on the train, looking under the seat for your ticket to tell you where you are going!

Reprogram Your Mind: The Light in the Barn

When we set goals in life, sometimes we may lose sight of them before they come to fruition. All of us start out with great intentions, but somehow we get lost along the way. We lose focus, get distracted or just plain scared, and give up on achieving those goals.

Sometimes this comes from a wish to go back to the safety and security of what we know. It feels safe to remain as we are. Change hints at danger on a certain level, and that is why we cling to what is familiar!

Do not beat yourself up because you have not achieved your goals. Instead, just reprogram your mind to achieve them. After all, you are master of your own mind! The mind has three parts: the conscious, the subconscious, and the creative subconscious.

Your conscious mind is where you perceive the world with your five senses. It is the place where you gather information. The conscious mind sorts and processes new information and delivers it to the subconscious.

The subconscious mind is a gigantic storehouse of information. Anything you have ever seen, heard, smelled, touched, tasted sensed, or thought is stored there. The subconscious stores your habits, your attitudes, and your version of the truth. Whenever new information enters the subconscious mind, it is associated with stored information and past experiences.

Let's say that you were warned repeatedly as a child to run if you ever saw a bear in the woods. Then one day, as an adult, you are walking in the woods, and you see a bear. Your conscious mind perceives the bear and reaches down into the subconscious mind for an evaluation. The subconscious associates the bear with your childhood training, and instantly you to take off running. You have no choice about the matter because you have been programmed by your subconscious mind.

Your creative subconscious maintains sanity, resolves problems, and produces energy and drive. When your conscious mind sets a goal and submits it to the subconscious mind for storage, the creative subconscious, by association, evaluates the goal for sanity.

If your beliefs about your life that have been stored in your creative subconscious do not match your goal, your creative subconscious will reject it as insane. Let's say you read one day that the way to react to a bear in the woods is to lie down and play dead. Your creative subconscious will reject that information as insane because it does not match your truth, stored in your subconscious mind.

To change anything in your world you must first change your stored version of the truth. An image of yourself achieving the goal you have set must be imbedded in your subconscious mind as a new version of the truth, and that new image must be larger than the images that preceded it there.

The way to reprogram your subconscious mind is through affirmations. An affirmation is a statement or belief that you repeat to yourself until it becomes part of your subconscious mind. You learn by repetition, and you can reprogram your subconscious through repetition. You must simply tell your subconscious mind, again and again and again, to associate the new image with the goal. It is just like reprogramming your image of what to do if you see a bear.

If you want to be wealthy, you must reprogram your subconscious to believe that you are worthy of wealth. If you want to lose weight, you must reprogram your subconscious to believe you should be lighter. If you want to sell more products next month, you must reprogram your subconscious to believe that you are capable of selling more.

Reprogramming your brain involves your emotions, images, and words. You have to be emotionally connected to your goal. Feel it, enjoy it, and revel in what your world would be like if you achieved it. Then create images that reflect exactly what your world will be like when you achieve your goal. Place those images in your house, and use them as a reminder to yourself of that goal every day. Write out exactly what your life will be like when you achieve your goal. Then discuss the possibilities with people you trust. Through repetition, you can create a new picture of your world inside your mind.

Once the internal picture of your goal is stronger than the picture you have of the world around you, you will begin to move toward that goal. You cannot move forward toward a goal unless you can clearly picture it in your mind. Once you have reprogrammed your subconscious mind you can do anything.

When I was a boy, one of my chores was to feed the horses each evening. Because I was only eight years old, I would often forget, and then my father would have to remind me,

"Have you fed the horses yet?" he would ask.

"No, sir. Do I have to? It's dark, and I'm afraid to go to the barn in the dark." I would always reply.

Our barn was a modern wood structure with a metal covering. It had electricity, running water, a feed room, and a tack room and was located about two hundred feet from our back door. It was just behind a thicket of white pines that my mother had planted for the purpose of hiding the barn from view.

One evening I asked my usual question: "Aw, Daddy, do I have to go feed the horses tonight?"

"Yes, you do," he answered. "It's your responsibility. You are depending on your mother and me to feed you each night. What would happen if one night we forgot or just did not feel like feeding you? How would you like to go to bed without food or water? You are responsible for the horses just like we are responsible for you. I know you are scared of the dark, so I will help you tonight."

Relieved, I headed for the back door with my father close behind me. It was going to be easy walking to the barn with him. When we got to the back door, he flicked on the lights in the carport, and we stepped outside.

"Go on to the barn. I will watch," Daddy said.

"Aren't you coming?" I asked, scared of what I knew his answer would be.

"No, I'll just watch."

So I headed off through the carport, out of the light, and into the darkness toward the barn, with my fear of the dark tightly gripping my little heart.

"Stop when you get to the edge of the light!" Daddy yelled.

I stopped at the edge of the white pines where the shadows fell and where blackness was all around, and I yelled back, "I'm at the edge of the light!"

"Can you see me standing in the carport light?"

"Yes."

"Can you see the barn in the dark?"

"No. There's not enough light."

"Do you know that the barn is there? Do you know that there's a light in the barn? Can you picture it in your mind?"

"Yes."

"Do you think it disappeared just because you can't see it in the dark?"

"No."

"Okay, continue to walk in the dark and just know the barn is there. The barn has not disappeared or changed just because you cannot see it. Have faith in yourself. When you get to the barn, you will find the light switch right there where it always is. All you have to do is turn on the lights. Then you will be able to see everything you need to see. "

I turned with the conviction of my father's words ringing in my ears and walked through the dark to the barn. I found the light switch and turned it on, flooding the barn with light. The horses — Lady, my sister Mary's small red quarter horse, and Bit-O-Honey, my big palomino mare — were there in their stalls. They had come in from the pasture and were waiting patiently for me to feed them. They made hunkering noises when they saw me, saying thanks for the food and water they were about to receive.

Nothing had changed. The barn was still there. The horses were still there. The feed room, tack room, saddles and bridles were just as I had envisioned them. The light revealed everything. I had reached my goal.

"See?" shouted my father when he saw the barn lights come on. "The barn is there, just like I said it would be. Congratulations on reaching your goal! Now, don't forget to give the horses some hay too." And he turned and went back into the house.

I remember walking through the dark to that barn many nights after my father died, hearing his words ringing in my head. "Continue to walk in the dark, just knowing the barn is there. The barn has not disappeared or changed just because you cannot see it. Have faith in yourself. When you get to your goal in life, just like the barn, you will find the light switch right there. All you have to do is turn on the lights. Then you will be able to see everything you need to see."

What have you lost in the darkness? What goal have you allowed to slip from your grasp because you did not fix a picture of it firmly in your mind? What have you not accomplished because you stopped moving forward in the darkness of life?

If you have set a goal but lost it in the darkness, do not get scared and turn back toward the light of what you know. Continue to walk ahead in the darkness. Your goal is there and has not changed just because you cannot see it in the dark. And when you arrive at the goal, you will find a light there that will light up your world. You can simply switch on that light and see how everything you have imagined has become real.

By making me feed the horses every night my father instilled in me the lesson of goal setting and having faith in myself. When you find that you have lost your way in the darkness of life, reevaluate your goals, and remember: there is always a light in the barn.

Give Yourself One Hour a Day: The Boy and the Coal Basket

My mother was an avid reader. She always kept books on her bedside table to read. She was always quoting a book about something. She read books on business, philosophy, economics, religion, and life. She was never very far from a book.

Late in life, when she lost her sight, my sister Mary would order audio books for Mother to "read." Then after she passed away, the North Carolina Library for the Blind told us that she had read four hundred audio books during the last eighteen months of her life!

All of us need to read more. It is estimated that half of the people in the United States today never read another entire book after high school! My mother always said that "a person who will not read is the same as a person who cannot read."

Take a moment to think about your reading. When was the last time you read a book? What was it about? Did it improve your life? Look at your day, and find one hour to devote to reading. Stop at your local book store and see what's happening. Not only are they filled with books, music, and magazines to make your life better, but now they also have food and drinks inside to keep you from getting hungry while you read!

Give yourself one hour a day to read. You could read a book every week. If you read a book every week, you would complete fifty-two books a year or 520 books during the next ten years. If you read 520 books in the next ten years, think how smart you would be. If you read books about sales, marketing, personal mastery, business development, technology and self improvement, you would be in the top one-tenth of one percent of your industry!

Begin and end each day reading. A friend of mine spends his lunch hour reading, uninterrupted, at his desk. You could listen to audio books in the car traveling to and from work and around town. Don't let something like "I don't have time" or "I can't see" stop you from reading. It didn't stop my mother!

There was an old man who lived on a farm in the mountains of eastern Kentucky with his young grandson. Each morning, the grandfather was up early, sitting at the kitchen table reading a book. His grandson, who wanted to be just like him, tried to imitate him by reading a book every morning too.

One day the grandson said, "Papa, I try to read just like you, but I don't understand very much, and what I do understand, I seem to forget as soon as I close the book. What good does reading do?"

The grandfather quietly turned away from adding coal to the stove and said, "I will answer your question in a minute but before I do please take this coal basket down to the river, and bring it back filled with water."

The boy did as he was told and all the way home water leaked out of the basket. When he finally arrived back at the house, his grandfather just laughed at the empty basket and said, "You'll have to move a little faster next time. Go back to the river with the basket and try again."

This time the boy ran faster, but again the basket was empty long before he reached the house. Out of breath, he told his grandfather that it was impossible to carry water in a basket and headed off to get a bucket instead.

The old man said, "I don't want a bucket of water, I want a basket of water. You can do this! You are just not trying hard enough." And he went outside to watch his grandson try again.

The boy knew that it was impossible to carry water in a basket, but he wanted to show his grandfather that he was willing to try. So he scooped up the water and ran hard, but when he reached his grandfather, the basket was, of course, empty again. Out of breath, he said, "See, Papa? It's useless!"

"So you think it's useless? Look at the basket."

Then the boy looked at the basket, and for the first time he realized that it looked different. Instead of a dirty old basket covered in coal dust, it was clean. All the water that had been running through the basket had left it clean.

That is what happens when you read! You may not understand or remember everything, but reading will change you from the inside out.

Your Strength of Purpose: Debt Free by November Three

My friend Ed Hatch is a great speaker. He travels the world teaching REALTORS® how to improve their real estate business. One of Ed's favorite quotes is by E.M. Gray: "**Successful people have the habit of doing things that failures don't like doing. *They* don't like doing them either, necessarily, but their disliking is subordinated to their *strength of purpose*.**"

If you are master your own life, then you must have the strength of purpose to do those things that other people just will not do. Identifying your strength of purpose in life will help you focus on what is important to you.

For example, you go to work because you need to earn money to feed your children. In this case, your strength of purpose is not the work itself but the need to provide food for your children. The stronger that purpose, the more likely you are to accomplish your task.

Knowing your strength of purpose helps keep you focused. When you clearly define your purpose, you can accomplish anything! I cannot give you a purpose for your life, only you can do that. I can only give you an example of how a strong purpose can change your life.

After fifteen years as a REALTOR®, I opened my own real

estate company. At the same time, unfortunately, Fort Bragg, our area's largest employer, began to downsize. Everyone was selling their house and moving somewhere else. No one was buying. The housing market was dead. I could not have picked a worse time to start a real estate company. We lost money from the very first day.

After a couple of years, I found myself in debt and struggling to make ends meet. I sought help from my local bank, but they turned me down. I went to a trusted friend, who loaned me enough money to escape from this financial crisis. I closed the company and began to start over financially. Over the next few years, I was able to repay only small portions of the loan.

My mother always worried about the debt I owed. It was important to her that I repay it because my father had once loaned a friend some money. The man refused to repay the loan after my father died. Mother made me promise that I would repay my debt, no matter what. My purpose was set and it was bound by that promise to my mother.

I struggled over the next few years to earn enough money to support my family and repay the loan. It would have been easier to forget the debt, of course, but I couldn't because I had promised my mother. *My strength of purpose was too strong to accept failure.*

Finally, I pledged myself to be debt-free on November third of the next year. To the mirror in my bathroom I attached a deposit slip dated November third that represented all the money I owed. I committed myself to travel all over the United States that year, speaking so that I could earn enough money to repay the entire loan.

I wanted my children to be part of the process of repaying the loan. I wanted them to understand that, if this debt was going to be repaid, we would all have to sacrifice. I would miss a lot of Cameron's little league games, and I would not be able to be there every time Louisa sang. I would be gone from home more than I wanted to, but if I was going to repay that loan, then that was what had to happen. My strength of purpose to repay the loan was stronger than my commitment to be present at my children's events.

I worked harder that year than ever before. I held a job at home and traveled to speak and teach every chance I got. There were times when I would take off in an airplane and not know what city I had just left or where I was going. I slept in hotels and ate in airports. I became exhausted and road-weary, but I kept going.

Several times I wanted to quit and go home, but I could not because my strength of purpose kept me going. As November third approached, I had to go to San Francisco for one more speaking engagement, and the kids and I delivered the last payments on the debt before I left. Because some of the money owed to *me* was late arriving — you know, "the check is in the mail" – one of the checks that we delivered had to be held until I could make a bank deposit. Luckily, our bene-factor agreed to hold *our* check until I called him.

After my speaking engagement in San Francisco, I went to Sausalito to celebrate paying off the debt. On November second my daughter called to say that the check we had been waiting for had arrived and been deposited in our bank ac-count. I immediately called the man who had loaned me the money and told him to deposit our check. I was debt-free on November third. I had kept my promise to my mother.

Did I want to quit? Yes. Had I wanted to give up? Yes. Had I ever thought that I would not make it? You bet! Every time I faltered, every time I thought I couldn't make it, I would remember my promise to my mother and keep going. E.M. Gray was right. My strength of purpose was strong enough to make me successful.

I treasure a photograph that was taken during my phone call from Sausalito. The photo captured me telling my benefactor that our check was good and the debt had been paid. The caption on the photograph reads:

Lunch at the Sausalito Restaurant $32.56

Sausalito sweatshirt $54.00

Reaching a goal to be debt-free by November third
Priceless

What keeps you going when there is no light at the end of the tunnel? If your strength of purpose is strong enough, you can endure whatever is necessary to accomplish your goal. You may not like doing it, but you will continue until you succeed.

Having a clearly defined purpose will help you become master of your own life.

Only *you* can define your purpose and only you can decide how strong that purpose is. Take a few moments to think about what is really important to you. What are you working for, really? What gets you up in the morning and keeps you working late at night? What makes you do things that you might not necessarily want to do otherwise?

To help you identify your purpose, write a list of the things that matter most to you and why. Put photos of those things up in your home and office, where you can be reminded of your purpose every day. Once you have clearly defined your purpose and determined how strongly you are committed to it, you will be the master of your life.

Know Yourself, and the Truth Will Set You Free!: Are You a Carrot, an Egg, or a Coffee Bean?

Uncle Adrian used to say "know yourself and the truth will set you free." Most people are limited by their self-perception. The formula for what they think they are supposed to receive in life is their abilities + their experience + their training + their personal appearance + their past + the expectations of others = their assigned territory in life

If you are bound by your self-perception, then you'd better identify what your self-perception *is* and work to expand it for the better.

A young woman went to her mother to tell her about her life and how things were so hard for her. She did not know how she was going to make it and wanted to give up. She was tired of fighting and struggling. It seemed that whenever one problem was solved, a new one arose.

So the mother took her daughter into the kitchen, filled three pots with water, and turned all three on to boil. In the first pot she placed carrots, in the second she placed eggs and in the last she placed ground coffee beans. Without saying a word, she let them sit and boil. In a few minutes she turned off the burners, poured out the carrots, eggs and coffee, placing them into separate bowls.

Turning to her daughter, she said, "Tell me what you see."

"Carrots, eggs, and coffee," the daughter replied.

The mother pulled her daughter closer and asked her to touch the carrots, which she did, noting that they were soft. Then she asked her to take the egg and break it, which she also did, observing that it was hard-boiled. Finally, she asked her daughter to smell and sip the coffee, which she did, smiling at its rich aroma. The daughter then asked, "So what's the point, Mother?"

Her mother explained "Each of these objects faced the same adversity — boiling water — but each reacted differently. The carrot had gone in strong, hard, and unrelenting. However, after being subjected to the boiling water, it became soft and weak. The egg had been fragile, with a thin outer shell protecting its liquid interior — until the boiling water had hardened the inside. The ground coffee beans, however, were unique. When placed in boiling water, *they had changed the water!*"

"Which are you?" the mother asked. "When trials and adversity knock on your door, how do you respond? Are you a carrot, an egg, or a coffee bean?"

Are you a carrot that seems strong until pain and adversity drain you of your strength? Are you the egg that begins life passively but changes with the heat? Did you have a fluid spirit until a death, a financial crisis, or some other trial toughened you? Does your shell look the same even though on the inside, you are bitter and tough, with a stiff and hardened spirit? Or are you like the coffee bean? The bean actually changes the very circumstance that brings it pain! When the water gets hot, instead of negatively altering the coffee bean, it releases the fragrance and flavor. If you are like the bean, you are at your best when the things around you are at their worst. When your trials seem insurmountable, do you elevate to another level?

How do you handle adversity — like the carrot, the egg, or the coffee bean?

Living in Harmony with the Unseen Order of Things: Seat 25-D

I was stuck in seat 25-D at the back of an airplane, exactly where I did not want to be. Oh, I got the seat I deserved — just not the one I wanted.

I had finished a long week of travel in California. I tried to fly home early to enjoy the weekend with my family but was disappointed to learn that all the airlines were booked. I had to stay overnight. The hotel room was not what I had expected. The heater in the room did not work so I shivered all night. The comforter smelled like aftershave. By 4:30 am, the cold room and the oppressive aftershave drove me to the lukewarm shower, and I got dressed for my day.

I worked on my computer until 6:00 am, when my breakfast was supposed to be delivered, though naturally it was late. I choked down the meal, and rushed for the airport shuttle. Too late I realized I had locked my cell phone in the room. The front desk was less than concerned with my problems, so I was furious!

Now I found myself sitting in seat 25-D, and it was entirely my fault. I just could not get out of my own way that morning and live in harmony with the unseen order of things. I just could not see the world as it was.

I could have called the front desk to have Management fix the heater. I could have asked for another blanket during the night. I could have ordered breakfast earlier. But no! I could not get out of my own way.

The universe will send you messages to lead you toward where you ought to be, but you have to be calm enough to listen. Usually, it is that little voice in your own head that says, "Calm down! This is not important." But we do not listen. We just cannot get out of our own way.

The universe sent me a big message that morning, but I could not quiet my mind enough to hear it. When I was standing at the front desk, impatiently expecting someone to retrieve my cell-phone, another man approached the counter to check out. His head, shoulders, arms, and torso were normal in size, but his legs were about eighteen inches long. In fact, he was barely taller than my suitcase. While I fumed, he quietly paid his bill and left.

I should have realized right then that my petty problems were not important, but I was so angry that I could not live in the harmony of the universe. I should have listened to the message that said, "Get over yourself, and enjoy the day. You could be *that* man!" But I just could not get out of my own way.

So I simmered all the way to the airport, through Security, and to the gate. The flight was oversold, but I managed to get the isle seat I had been assigned – 8-B, at the front of the plane. Nevertheless, I was still angry when I sat down.

It looked as if I might have two seats all to myself, but at the last minute I heard arguing from the front of the plane, and then an angry couple approached. They stopped at my row.

"We were supposed to sit together," the woman whined, looking at me as if I were something that had just crawled out from under a rock, "but the airline lied to us. Would you help out by taking my husband's seat in the rear of the plane?" And, coming from her mouth, those words constituted a demand, not a question!

Now, I am normally very accommodating, but in this case I was still upset from the morning's events, so I replied, "I will certainly move as long as I am moving to an aisle seat." I do not like window seats, and I was not about to inconvenience myself any further. I had already had a terrible morning. I *deserved* to sit in the seat I had chosen. I just could not get myself out of my own way.

"It's a window seat," she said menacingly.

"Then no, I will not move."

Now the woman was not happy with me *or* the airline. When she sat down beside me, she made sure I knew just how disgruntled she was by huffing and puffing and turning every page of her magazine with an angry jerk. When a passenger in the row behind us began to open up some food for her child, she made lots of noise taking off the cellophane wrapper. The woman beside me turned and glared at them over the seat back because they were disturbing her. What a grouch!

She was acting as if the entire world were upsetting her. She was acting like an idiot. She was acting just like I had that morning in the hotel!

I tried to ignore her by getting my laptop out of its case as soon as I could. However, my neighbor was not to be ignored! As soon as I had the computer open, my headphones on and had settled down to work, she said, "I have to get out!" and began to shove me out of my seat.

After she left, I was relieved to have peace descend on my little corner of the world. My relief quickly turned to frustration, however, when she sent her husband to tell me that they had found me an aisle seat at the back of the plane! She had rearranged everyone on row 25 just so that she could sit with her husband in my row! Being a man of my word I had no other choice but to move.

Now, sitting in seat 25-D, I have come to realize that my early-morning actions probably caused my difficulties here on the airplane. If I had been kinder to the hotel staff and recognized my stupidity in trying to hold *them* responsible for *my* actions, I would probably be sitting in 8-B beside a supermodel! But instead I had acted like an idiot this morning, and the universe had delivered into my life the absolutely obsessed woman in the seat next to mine — just so that I could see what I had looked like earlier in the day.

What you give to the universe, you will get back. I know, because I gave frustration and anger that day, and that is exactly what I got back. As Uncle Adrian always said, "What goes around comes around." We're all connected to the same universe.

What are you missing every day because you do not live in harmony with the unseen order of things? What messages are you ignoring every day even though listening to them would make your life better?

Life lived in fear and frustration cuts you off from the universe. You cannot see or hear the messages that life is sending to you when you are distracted by impatience, bitterness, or anger.

If you live in harmony with the unseen order of things you will discover an order to the universe. Your responsibility in life is to find that order and live within it. When you do that, you will realize that the universe is a fabulous adventure just waiting for you.

Besides, you do not want to spend all your time flying at the back of the plane, do you?

PART THREE

Relationships

Uncle Adrian and his wife, Myrtle Reid

"You become who you hang out with."

Uncle Adrian

Managing Disappointment: Good or Bad? We Will See

Some years ago I met two extraordinary women, Allison Mooney and Beverly Steiner, through the good fortune of being a speaker for the Council of Residential Specialists (CRS), a division of the National Association of REAL-TORS®. At CRS we presented two-day business-training programs to the top three percent of all REALTORS®.

At one point in her speaking career, Allison was faced with a huge disappointment. None of us knew how to console her, but Beverly came to the rescue with a poignant letter. If you have ever pursued something, only to have it barred from your reach at every turn then this story is right for you. It's from a letter that Beverly sent to Allison after her heartbreaking disappointment.

> Dear Allison,
>
> After I left Chicago today, I found myself searching for what words of wisdom I might have had for you as we discussed your disappointment, but nothing came to mind. It occurred to me that everything I might have said would somehow have been wrong.
>
> So here I sit on the plane flying home, reading a magazine I bought at the hotel today. And in the final

paragraphs of the final story in this magazine is the message I was searching for earlier. I do not believe it was a coincidence that this story is so right, and at such an appropriate moment! I believe it was given to me so that I could pass it on to you. It reads as follows:

"For thirty days I trekked through South Korea with my Buddhist Zen master, climbed mountains, and ran to catch buses in ninety-degree humidity — all while wearing heavy gray robes. I got no more than five hours sleep a night and ate meals of just rice, vegetables, and maybe a little protein. It was a month of furniture-less rooms and sleeping on floor mats after carrying a twenty-pound backpack containing books that monks and nuns had given my teacher along the way. The journey devastated me because I had expected my teacher to be the gentle, funny — the direct mentor I thought I knew. Instead, he became frustrated with my exhaustion and angry at my igno-rance of local customs. It was like losing a best friend from a thousand lifetimes. All that without candy, makeup, or hair stuff.

"And I am thankful for all of it. The pilgrimage forced me to trust myself in the deepest sense of the word, and in the middle of that trust I discovered compas-sion — compassion for myself and for my teacher. I had to let go of everything I had hoped the journey would be: sweet, slow walks in the woods with breaks for tea and lively conversation. Instead, the trip was so raw that it forced me to stop yearning for a world where life is exactly what I want it to be...and accept what life is. In the letting go, gratitude showed up.

"There is a Zen story about a man who, when his horse runs away, says, 'Good or bad? We will see.' When the horse returns with several wild horses, and his son wants to celebrate, the father repeats the phrase. 'Good or bad? We will see.' The son then breaks his leg trying to tame one of the wild horses, but not until the injury keeps him from going to war does he realize his father's reluctance ever to celebrate or to mourn. 'Good or bad? We will see.'"

"It is hard to know, at any given moment, what to be grateful for. Sometimes it is easy to feel great pools of gratitude — for fresh fall days, for the people we love. Other times it is almost impossible. But then we wait. 'Good or bad? We will see.'"

And that, Allison my friend, would have been what I would have wanted to say. We do not know why, but it is the journey that is most important, not the destination. It is best to detach ourselves from the outcome and let life take us where we need to be. You need to be on this journey for some reason, Allison. It may be for some of the reasons you talked to me about today. This day for you, and this day for me, "Good or bad? We will see..."

Stay detached from the outcome, my friend, and you will never be disappointed. Let your spiritual path unfold as it needs to. You know — above all else, that is the point of everything we do. I will say what I know for certain: you and I were meant to be friends. To me, that is the most important part of this journey so far. Everything else — "Good or bad? We will see..."

Beverly

Have you ever been disappointed? Have you ever wanted to achieve something, only to find out that you could not have it? Do you think that we are on this earth to be denied the things that we are working for? I do not think so!

Stop and think for a moment about your life. Can you imagine a place better suited for learning about life than this earth? Why are you here, if not to achieve mastery in your own life? Do not be disappointed if things are not going your way right now because what comes next could be good, or it could be bad. Hang in there, and you will see.

Allison Mooney responded to this story by saying, "I want

people to realize that the journey does not end and that much good has happened to me as a result of letting go and heading down a different path. God does not always grant our prayer requests the way we desire. He sometimes says 'no' when we desperately want Him to say 'yes.' Letting go is one of the most difficult tasks anyone can experience. It was *extremely* difficult for me. You see, the disappointment I experienced was part of a ten-year goal. But now my goal and plan in life have taken a huge and wondrous turn! Every day is a new experience! It is a life of learning, growing, and becoming. It is a life of meeting extraordinary people and reading new books. Let go, and live! You will never cease to be amazed!"

Good or bad? We will see.

Toxic People: The Bad Hair Day

Most people are good. Uncle Adrian would say that, if you give them a chance in life, they will show you their goodness. However, he would also tell you that "every now and then you will meet a mean, nasty, ugly person. Of course, the problem with mean, nasty, ugly people is that they move around a lot, and you keep bumping into them!"

I call them "toxic people." They poison life for everyone they meet. You know who they are. They are the people who make you miserable, and you keep bumping into them!

Lots of times these people appear to be congenial and sincerely interested in you, but when you scratch the surface, you will discover that they are toxic. That is why Uncle Adrian would always tell the story about the bad hair day...

A woman was at her hairdresser's getting her hair styled for a trip to Rome that she would soon be making with her husband. When she mentioned her plans her hairdresser asked, "Rome? Why would anyone want to go there? It is crowded and dirty. You are crazy to go to Rome! How on earth are you getting there?"

"We are flying," the woman replied. "We got a great rate!"

"What airline?" asked the hairdresser. "That is a terrible

choice," he said when she told him. "Their planes are old, their flight attendants are ugly, and they are always late. So where are you staying in Rome?"

"We will be at this exclusive little place right on the Tiber River. It is called Teste."

"Do not go any further. I know the Teste! Everybody thinks it is going to be something special and exclusive, but it is really a dump — the worst hotel in the city! The rooms are small, the staff is surly, and the place is overpriced. So what are you planning to do once you get there?"

"We are going to the Vatican, and we are really hoping to see the Pope."

"That is rich!" laughed the hairdresser. "You and a million other people will be trying to see him. He will look the size of an ant! So good luck on this lousy trip of yours, you are going to need it!"

A month later when the woman came in again to have her hair done, the hairdresser asked about her trip to Rome.

"It was wonderful!" exclaimed the woman. "Not only was our flight on time it was in one of their brand new planes! Because the main cabin had been overbooked, we were bumped up to First Class. The food and wine were spectacular, and I had a handsome twenty-eight-year-old steward who waited on me hand and foot."

"The hotel was perfect! The owners had just finished a five-million-dollar remodeling job, and now the place is a jewel — the finest establishment in the city. The hotel was over-booked too, so the Manager apologized and gave us the owner's suite at no extra charge!"

"Well," muttered the hairdresser, "that is all well and good, but I know you did not get to see the Pope."

"Actually, we were quite lucky about that too! As we were touring the Vatican, a Swiss Guard tapped me on the shoulder. When I turned around, he explained that since the Pope likes to meet some of his visitors personally, my husband and I were being invited to step into his office for a private audience. Sure enough, in walked the Pope five minutes later and shook my hand! Even though I was in a state of utter shock, I knelt down before him, and he spoke a few words to me."

"Oh, really? What did he say?"

He said, "Where did you get that awful hairdo?"

If you read Scott Peck's book *People of the Lie,* you will learn that toxic people are just hiding from themselves. Since they are not happy in their own lives, they are always trying to stop everybody else from being happy. Their only joy comes from ruining someone else's chances for happiness.

You should remove toxic people from your life. Toxic people are like poison in your food. In any contest between food and poison, the poison will always win. Make a list of the people in your life who are toxic for you. Include everybody who makes you feel sad or confused when you are around them. Now work to remove these people from your life.

Then create a second list. This is a list of all the people who add value to your life just by being in it. Include everyone who has helped you achieve your goals. Work hard to keep the good people in your life. Life is too short to be spent around people who do not enhance the adventure for you.

Besides, you can always get somebody else to do your hair!

Love Creates Value:
The Note in the Glove Box

Life is all about relationships. In fact, nothing is more important than becoming master of the relationships in your life. If you have everything in the world but do not have love, you have nothing.

I think Laura Arch summed it up best when she said, "All we want is a peaceful, trusting, and loving relationship filled with laughter." How good can your life be when you love, and are loved by, someone else?

Uncle Adrian was driving to work one day and had a fender bender. When the woman in the other car got out, she was crying hysterically. "Look," Uncle Adrian said, trying to be helpful, "it's not that bad of an accident, and I'm sure your insurance will cover the damage."

"You don't understand!" she sobbed. "This is my husband's dream car! He worked for years to earn the money to buy it. It is his passion! This car is everything to him, and we just got it three days ago! He will be furious that I wrecked it!"

"I'm sure that he will understand," said Uncle Adrian, "but right now I'm in a hurry to get to work, so let's just exchange insurance information and phone numbers."

The woman went to her car to get the insurance card in the glove box and found a large manila envelope containing all the registration and insurance information. When she opened it and removed its contents the first thing she saw was a letter-sized envelope with the following words, OPEN FIRST IN CASE OF AN ACCIDENT, written in her husband's handwriting.

With trembling hands, she opened the envelope. Inside was a note from her husband that said, "Honey, in case of an accident, remember that it is you I love – not the car!"

What do you love? Do you love the people in the car more than the car itself? Love is truly the most powerful thing in life. Find the people and the things you love, and you will also find your calling in life. Mastery of your life will flow from your love.

"And now these three remain: faith, hope, and love. But the greatest of these is love" (Corinthians 13:13, The Holy Bible, New International Version.)

Your Point of View:
Beverly on the Beach

My friend Beverly Steiner, finding herself with a half day to spend in Hawaii before flying home, decided to head for the beach. With her lunch and a good book, she settled herself on the sand.

Almost immediately, she realized that a huge storm cloud was brewing over the ocean, right in front of her. Just below that angry cloud was a boat full of people. When the rain began to fall all the people on the boat scurried for cover.

Back on the beach where Beverly was sitting, the sun was shining, flowers were blooming, and life was good.

To her right a festive group was assembling on the beach. A bride and groom with their family and friends gathered to get married. They were about to celebrate the most joyous day in their lives.

Back on the beach where Beverly was sitting, the sun was shining, flowers were blooming, and life was good.

Then she noticed a couple on a beach blanket to her left, close enough for her to overhear their conversation. Of course, it isn't hard to distinguish everything that two people are saying when they are shouting at each other! Apparently, they had come to Hawaii to rekindle the fire in their relationship. Instead the wife had found out about her husband's extramarital affair and confronted him on the beach. It was the last day of their vacation, and it was ugly.

Back on the beach where Beverly was sitting, the sun was shining, flowers were blooming, and life was good.

Beverly thought about her strange day on the plane ride home. All three groups of people had been on the same beach at the same time, yet each would remember that day with different memories.

The people on the boat would report that they had had a stormy day and been drenched with rain. The newlyweds would look back on their perfect ceremony and cherish the memory of it always. The couple shouting over the husband's affair would think of that time and place and remember how their disintegrating marriage had finally come to an end.

Beverly would remember it as the day when she learned that everything in life depends on your point of view. A world full of people can share an experience, but it is how you *react* to the experience that creates your reality.

PART FOUR

The Value of Joy!

Uncle Adrian Modeling in a Fashion Show

"Cast your bread upon the water and it will come back with a weenie and mustard."

Uncle Adrian

Your To-Do List:
One Thousand Saturdays

Do you have a list of things that you want to do in your lifetime? I'm not talking about everyday, normal things, but great things. Adventuresome things like climbing mountains, swimming in all the worlds seas or discovering life on another planet. Have you compiled a list of the most important things you'd like to do in your life so that you can look it over daily and remember exactly what those dreams are? Start on that list today!

"Oh, I stopped dreaming long ago," you may say. Exactly the problem! You stopped dreaming! You should never stop dreaming! You should never stop learning! Never stop believing that life is a great adventure!

My good friend Betty Wilson sent me a Christmas card this past year telling me all about how she had gone back to college to get another degree and start a new career. When she showed up for her first class, everyone seemed to know her name. The professor announced to the students that there was a celebrity in their midst. When Betty looked around to see who this famous person could possibly be, she discovered that everybody was looking directly at her! The professor said that everybody should be honored to have her there because she was the oldest person ever enrolled in the college. Betty is seventy, starting a new career and she made the highest grades of any student in her class!

When I called my best friend the other day, he was on his way to his violin lesson. There is nothing so unusual about that...except that he's fifty years old and has never played any musical instrument! So I asked him what in the world he was doing, and he said, "Living the life I've always dreamed about!"

What dreams did you have as a child or young adult that you have forgotten or abandoned along the bumpy road of life? You are never too old to dream.

I stopped by Uncle Adrian's office one day to complain about my all-work, no-adventure life, and he said, "It sounds as if you're too busy working to have any fun. I am sure they pay you well, but it is a shame that you have to be away from your home and family so much. It's just really hard to believe that someone would need to work sixty or seventy hours a week. Too bad you're missing out on the great adventure of life, but I guess you are just trying to make enough money to enjoy yourself!" Then he said, "Let me tell you about something that's helped me find balance in my life.

"You see, I sat down one day and did a little arithmetic. The average person lives about seventy-five years. So I multiplied seventy five times fifty two weeks per year and came up with three thousand nine hundred. This is the number of Saturdays in an average person's lifetime.

"Now, stick with me because I'm getting to the important part.

It took me until I was fifty years old to think about all of this in any detail," he went on, "and by that time I had lived through more than twenty-six-hundred Saturdays. I got to thinking that, if I lived to be seventy-five, I had only about a thousand Saturdays left to enjoy.

"So I went to a toy store and bought a thousand marbles — every single marble they had. Then I took them home and placed them inside a clear plastic container. Every Saturday since then, I have taken out one marble and thrown it away. I have found that, by watching the marbles diminish, I have become more focused on the really important things in life. Knowing that there is a limited time for your life is a great inspiration because there is nothing like a deadline to help you get your priorities straight."

"I hope you will begin spending more time with your loved ones, and find the adventure in every Saturday you have left!" After I walked out of Uncle Adrian's office, I realized that he was right. Every day is a new adventure to look forward to.

So what are you planning for this coming Saturday? Will you share it with the really important people in your life? Are you going to start on one of your great adventures? Maybe you could have a picnic in the park or spend the evening catching fireflies with your children. Just do something that matters to you.

To help you get started, I want you to make a list of all the things you'd like to accomplish during your lifetime. Think of the six areas of mastery: physical, spiritual and educational, relationships, joy, business, and financial. Ask yourself what you would like to be. Ask yourself what you would like to do. And ask yourself what things you would like to have.

Once you have your list in hand, do not waste another moment of another day! Set about right then living the life you've always dreamed about. And while you're out on your adventures, you can stop at a toy store and buy some marbles!

Passion and Persistence: A Golfing Story

My best friend, G.L. Draughon, says, "Passion and persistence will overcome ability every time." He is right! I do not care what else you have going for you: passion and persistence will always win out.

When I was a USPTA Tennis Professional, I trained thousands of people to play the game. I worked with players at all skill levels, from beginners to professionals. Once I coached two boys, both of whom were good players, but one was the most gifted natural athlete I have ever worked with. Unfortunately, he had no passion or persistence as far as tennis was concerned. The other boy was not particularly gifted physically, but he worked at his tennis game with such passion and persistence that he became a top collegiate player.

Having the passion and persistence to master your life is important. In fact, it may be the most important thing. You may have talent, intelligence, education and breeding but none of those things will ever replace passion for what you do and persistence to finish what you start.

Uncle Adrian loved to tell the story of a good friend who was passionate about playing the game of golf. Nothing gave him more pleasure than taking friends and family members to the golf course to play.

One day he could not find anyone else to play golf with him so he asked his wife to play. He knew she would not play, but she could walk with him and enjoy the beautiful day. She agreed and they arrived at the course for their tee time early in the morning.

On the second green, his wife stepped into a hole and broke her ankle! The golfer was in a dilemma. His wife was a large woman, and the golfer was a small man, so carrying her would be an almost impossible task. He could not leave her to go for help, and he could barely pick her up. Finding no other solution to his problem, however, he hoisted her up.

Naturally, nobody in the clubhouse knew a thing about what had happened until Uncle Adrian's friend was spotted struggling up the fairway and onto the eighteenth green. Once they realized that he was carrying his wife, everyone watching rushed out to help.

As the dedicated golfer lowered his wife onto the green, everyone gathered around. "What an amazing feat of passion and persistence to carry your wife all the way from the second hole to the eighteenth green!" they exclaimed. "How did you do it?" someone asked.

"Well," the golfer began, "carrying my wife was not the

problem. Picking her up and putting her down between shots was the problem!"

What are you passionate about? Take the time to consider your passions in life, and then determine whether you will be persistent enough to follow those passions to their completion. If you are passionate and persistent, you will be able to accomplish anything you set your mind to. Never give up, and you will overcome any obstacles that you may find in your way.

What You Focus on Expands: Mr Phipps the Math Teacher

What you focus on expands in your life. Expect good, and it will come to you. Expect bad, and you will receive it.

How is that so, you ask? Well, you are equipped with a brain that filters out all those things you do not consider important. Once you program yourself to find good or bad, your brain will fulfill the task you have set it to.

Everything depends on what you are focused on. You can program yourself to be a success or a failure. You can program yourself to be happy or sad. You can program yourself to become master of your life or a victim of circumstances. Whatever you focus on expands.

At Central High School there was an exceptional math teacher named Mr. Phipps, who was greatly loved. He had taught several generations of students in Eastern Cumberland County. Eventually he retired and was living happily in his house off Dunn Road.

A few years after Mr. Phipps' retirement, the Central High principal called. He was faced with a dilemma: all the students in a senior class were failing math, and their teacher had transferred to another school in the middle of the year. To make matters worse, these were "problem students." Most of them were troublemakers, and the rest were expected to barely graduate and never go on to college. In a desperate move, the principal asked Mr. Phipps to return to school and take over this pathetic excuse for a math class.

To everyone's surprise, Mr. Phipps enthusiastically accepted the challenge. Under his guidance, the students worked hard, and at the end of the year, the entire class graduated — most of them with honors in math! As a matter of fact, their math scores were so high that many of these former losers went on to college!

At the end-of-the-year awards ceremony, the principal delivered a rousing speech about the wonderful job that Mr. Phipps had done in the midst of a very discouraging situation. He noted that most of the students had been considered academically challenged before Mr. Phipps had arrived on campus, but that everyone had made surprising progress under his tutelage.

When Mr. Phipps stood up to give his remarks, he responded by saying, "With the level of intelligence that these students had, teaching them was a challenging job, but I was up to the task. You see, when I arrived here, the principal gave me a list of the names of the students and their IQ scores. In all my years of teaching, I had never had an entire class of students with IQ scores that high, and I knew I was facing my smartest group of students ever."

"As a matter of fact, I carried that piece of paper with their IQ scores on it with me all year. I needed it to inspire me to keep ahead of that bunch of geniuses. I knew I would have to throw out the book and teach them the toughest math I could find in order to stay ahead of their ability to learn. I even contacted my friends who were math professors in college and got their help in advanced mathematics. Challenging these students was tough! In fact, I do not know why everybody's applauding me. These kids were so smart that they had to do well!

"I have the paper with me now, and I say again that I would have expected nothing less from the smartest class of my teaching career," said Mr. Phipps, waving the evidence over his head.

"Let me see that list!" demanded the principal, snatching it from Mr. Phipps' hand. Taking one incredulous look at it, he exclaimed, "This is not a list of their IQ's! This is a list of their locker numbers!"

You get what you expect from life. Expect the best from others, and you'll receive it. Expect the worst, and you'll find it everywhere.

Take a moment to think about how you are programming yourself. Do you constantly tell yourself you are not worthy of great things in life? Do you tell yourself you cannot? Do you tell yourself you are not capable?

All of us practice affirmations. Every one of us has an internal dialogue. What is your self- talk? What are you saying to yourself? Are you encouraging yourself to become master of your own life, or are you your own worst critic? It is time to pay attention to that internal conversation. You may be affirming the wrong things!

Begin today to affirm to yourself that you are worthy of great things in your life. Begin today to control your self-affirmations. Write down ten positive statements about yourself, and repeat them to yourself, out loud, several times a day. You will be reprogramming your mind.

I have a friend who records her affirmations on a digital recorder in her own voice and then plays them to herself as she drives to work every day. Sound crazy? No crazier than listening to the junk on the radio and not expecting it to affect your outlook on life!

Nelson Mandela said it this way; *"Our deepest fear is not that we are inadequate. Our deepest fear is that we are powerful beyond measure. It is our Light, not our Darkness, that most frightens us. We ask ourselves, 'Who am I to be brilliant, gorgeous, talented, and fabulous?' Actually, who are you not to be? You are a child of God. Your playing small doesn't serve the world. There is nothing enlightened about shrinking so the other people won't feel insecure around you. We are all meant to shine, as children do. We were born to make manifest the glory of God that is within us. It's not just in some of us; it's in everyone. And as we let our own light shine, we unconsciously give other people permission to do the same. As we are liberated from our own fear, our presence automatically liberates others."*

Start telling yourself that you are worthy! Convince yourself that you should be master of your own life, and you will see results.

And if you should ever have to take a math class, make sure that Mr. Phipps is your teacher!

Reticular Activating System:
You Become What You Think About

Dr. Roger Sperry won the Nobel Prize in 1982 for his research on how the human brain functioned. In fact, he developed many of the theories that we adhere to today about how the brain operates.

One of the interesting questions addressed by Dr. Sperry was that of the brain's capacity. He wanted to know exactly what percentage of our brains we use. He discovered that he could not calculate that percentage because he could not calculate the capacity of the human mind. He concluded that the mind's capacity was unlimited!

Dr. Sperry also discovered that our brains come equipped with the tools necessary for finding answers to any question. The Reticular Activating System (RAS) is a filter for information that is located at the base of your brain. It allows into your conscious awareness only those things which you have determined, in advance, to be important. When you clearly define what is important to you by creating written, visual, and emotional goals for your life, you put your Reticular Activating System to work for you. It will select, from the billions of messages that your mind receives every minute, the ones you have pre-determined as important. But you must clearly define what's important!

Stop for a moment to think of your dream car. Mine is a 1965 Corvette. Whatever your favorite car is, do you notice it when you pass one on the road? You don't notice all the cars on the road, just your favorites. That is your Reticular Activating System filtering out the other cars on the highway but allowing all the information about your favorite car to get through to you.

Another example is a mother sleeping at night, with her newborn baby in the next room. The mother can be sound asleep, and there can be other noises in the house, but she will wake up when she hears her baby's cry. It is not the volume of the baby's cry that activates the mother's Reticular Activating System. It is the importance that the mother attaches to the sound. Typically, the husband does not hear the baby crying in the night because his Reticular Activating System is programmed to filter out those sounds.

Your Reticular Activating System will provide you with the answers for mastering your life as long as you clearly define what is important to you. You were meant to be successful! You come equipped with all the tools necessary to be successful. You simply must define what you want from your life and allow the Reticular Activating System to filter out all the non important information and allow all the important answers to come into your conscious mind.

On the other hand, your brain is also wired to make you fail if you program it the wrong way. If you focus on your mistakes, you will make more mistakes. If you focus on your weaknesses, they will grow bigger. If you focus on why something will not work, sure enough, it will not work. Your brain will make sure of that!

"You become what you think about" Uncle Adrian told me one day when I stopped by Acme Fence Company to visit with him. I had heard him say that very same thing many times before but on that particular occasion it seemed to sink in. In fact, it kept ringing in my ears the rest of the day.

"You become what you think about." For a seventeen-year-old boy, that concept was disturbing! Could my thoughts really change me? Could I change my life just by thinking about something constantly?

"You become what you think about." Uncle Adrian's words kept on ringing in my ears. I couldn't sleep. I couldn't eat. I couldn't study. I could hardly drive my car!

"You become what you think about." I knew that I was in trouble because, if I was going to become what I thought about, I would soon be turning into a girl!

What do you think about? What are your thoughts focused on? Whatever you are focused on will soon appear in your life. What if you could program your brain to find the answers to all of life's problems? Well, you can!

Take a moment to list all the things that are important to you. Turn that list into photos, written words, and emotional messages to yourself. Become master of your Reticular Activating System, and allow into your consciousness everything that is important in your life.

Train your brain to work for you. After all, your Reticular Activating System is working all the time. If you're not the master of your own thoughts, who is? Remember -- you become what you think about!

PART FIVE

Mastery In Business

Uncle Adrian at his desk at Acme Fence Company, Fayetteville NC

"If it were easy, everybody would do it"

Uncle Adrian

Profit Is Better Than Wages: A Letter Home from Boot Camp

A great investment on your road to mastery is to start your own business. There are opportunities for you to start a business every day. In America, if you find a need, someone will pay you to provide a solution.

A hundred years ago, all of us owned our own businesses. We were the butchers, the bakers, and the candlestick makers. Today, we are taught to think that the best business decision would be to get a college degree and a nice job with benefits. Uncle Adrian knew that the safest choice you can make is to control your own destiny by starting a business.

Have you ever started a business? Do you have a product or service that could make money for you? Take a moment to examine the possibilities. What expertise do you have? What service or products would people pay you to provide?

A business exists to provide a service that consumers want so that it can charge a fee and make a profit for its owners. Profit is what is left after expenses are subtracted from income. If you spent thousands of dollars to go to the finest business school in the United States, here is what that school would teach you about running a business: Income minus Expenses equals Profit.

Profit is a good thing. If you make enough profit, you will be able to hire others who can make a living out of your business too. Your customers and clients will be happy because a profitable business can afford to provide excellent products and services. A profitable business attracts competition and creates a competitive marketplace where the ultimate winner is the consumer. Profit is good for everyone.

You may be afraid to open a business because you want the security of working for someone else, but working for someone else gives them control of your income and of your creative life! You are subject to their decisions. If they decide to make changes that you do not like, you will be stuck working in an environment that is not right for you, or you will have to seek another job.

If you are an employee of any business, you are at the mercy of the marketplace. If the marketplace no longer needs the products or services that your employer provides, the company will not make a profit. If there is no profit, you will have no job!

If you work for someone else and would like to be promoted to a better position with a higher salary, you will have to wait for someone who outranks you to be promoted, leave the company, or die. Do you want to wait till someone above you is promoted, leaves the company, or dies before you can better your position in life?

If you own your own business, on the other hand, you are in control of your own destiny. If you make a profit, you get to keep it! If you do not make a profit, you can cut expenses, rearrange your business model, change your products or services, or close the doors and walk away. No matter what happens, you are still in control of your own destiny.

Uncle Adrian started a business while he was in the U.S. Army during World War II, serving as a drill sergeant. He agreed to drive the other soldiers to town in his car on a Saturday night, guaranteeing them that even if they got drunk, he would get them back to the base on time. He charged each man five dollars for his service.

Uncle Adrian was a large man, about 6 feet 5 inches tall and because he was the drill sergeant, I am sure he was able to handle just about anything. He knew that he might have to fight his soldiers if they were drunk. The experience taught him that giving someone something that they needed was not always easy. He told me "the trick to that particular deal was that you had to get your five dollars in advance because they would spend all their money once they got into town."

Here is a letter that could have been written by one of Uncle Adrian's young recruits.

Dear Ma and Pa,
I'm well. Hope you are. Tell Brother Walt and Brother

Elmer that the Army beats working for old man McLaurin by a mile. Tell them to join up quick before all of the good places in the army are filled.

I was restless at first because I got to stay in bed till nearly 6 a.m., but now I'm getting so I like to sleep late.

Tell Walt and Elmer that all I do before breakfast is smooth my cot and shine my shoes. No hogs to slop, cows to feed, horses to catch, logs to split, or firewood to gather. There is almost nothing to do!

Breakfast is strong on the trimmings — like fruit juice, cereal, eggs, and bacon — but kind of weak on chops, potatoes, ham, steak, and other regular food. Tell Walt and Elmer, that they can always sit beside a couple of city boys who practically live on coffee. Their food plus yours will hold you till noon, when you finally get fed again.

Of course, without much food it's no wonder these city boys can't walk much! We go on something called "routine marches," which Sergeant Williams says are long walks to strengthen us and if he thinks so, it's not my place to tell him different. A "routine march" is about as far as to Bruce Williford's Store back home. Then the city guys get sore feet, and we all ride back to camp in trucks. The country is nice but awful flat.

Sergeant Williams is just like a school teacher. He barks and yells and nags us a lot, but I think he wants what's best for us. The Captain is a city boy and doesn't seem to know much. Majors and Colonels just ride around and look real serious. They don't bother us none.

This next part will make Walt and Elmer fall on the floor laughing. I keep getting medals for shooting, and I don't know why! The bulls-eye is near as big as a squirrel's head, and it don't move. It doesn't even shoot back, like the Horne boys do at home. All we got to do is lie there all comfortable and hit it.

Then we have what they call hand-to-hand combat training, where we get to wrestle with them city boys. I have to be real careful, though, because those fellows break easy. It ain't like fighting with that ole bull at home – I can tell you that! I'm about the best they got here except for that Franklin Johnson from over in Grey's Creek. I didn't beat him but once. He joined up the same time as me, but he's 6'8" and weighs near 300 pounds, while I'm only 5'6" and 130 pounds soaking wet.

Be sure to tell Walt and Elmer to hurry and join before too many other fellers catch on to this set-up and come stampeding in. Better go now. Sergeant Williams is hollering again.

Your loving daughter,

Gail

During the war Uncle Adrian worked for Uncle Sam during the week and for himself on the weekends. He could tell you that running your own business and making a profit was better than working for a company and earning a wage.

Consider starting your own business today. It could be as simple as giving someone a ride to town.

Know Your Customers:
Funeral for a Dog

Do you know your customers? I mean, really know them? Do you know what they think, how they live, where they shop, and what they buy? If you do, then you are in touch with the people who buy your goods and services. If not, you may be surprised to find your business losing money to other businesses that have studied your customers and are in touch with their wants and needs.

Demographics is the study of people — of what they do and how they live. Demographics can tell you everything from how often those people change the oil in their cars to how much toothpaste they buy in a year. There is great demographic research today for any product or service you can imagine.

In a small business, you can do research on every one of your customers. Simply ask each one what they want and whether they think you could do a better job providing your service or products. Most small businesses are afraid to ask their customers what the business could do for them. Some business owners do not what to hear the answers. However, if you understand that a business exists only to provide what the customer wants, then it would be ridiculous to operate your company in a communications vacuum.

When Uncle Adrian wanted to teach you something about customer research, he would tell you the story of a man who wanted a funeral for his dog.

You see, Uncle Adrian had a friend who sang in the choir of the Presbyterian Church and lived alone except for an old yellow Labrador retriever. The man and his dog were inseparable. Finally one day the old dog died and the man went to the church and asked the pastor to hold a funeral for him.

"What?" exclaimed the outraged preacher. "This is the Presbyterian Church. We are known as the finest church in town! Only the best people attend our services. We do not give funerals for dogs here! Why don't you go down the road to the Baptist church? They might hold a funeral for your dog."

"Well," replied the man, "I certainly understand you not wanting to conduct a funeral for my dog. I was going to donate $75,000 to the church in the dog's name after the funeral."

"Oh!" exclaimed the preacher. "You didn't tell me that your dog was a Presbyterian!"

Knowing who your customers are will help you serve their needs better. Targeting those customers who really want and need your goods or services will save you marketing money.

Stop for a moment to think about your customer. Who exactly are your customers? How do they think? How do they live, work, and play? How does your product or service fit into their lives? How will you contact them, and how often do they need you? Spend some time talking with your customers, and you will discover what they want.

Then you better check to see whether they have an old yellow dog that go everywhere with them. You just might want to provide services for their pets too!

Larry Kendall: Mastery

Larry Kendall, CEO of The Group, Inc., a real estate firm in northern Colorado introduced me to the term "mastery." His influence along with that of Walt Frey has propelled me to a higher state of mastery in my own life.

Larry Kendall is a rarity in today's business world for several reasons. First, he is extremely well read. Whenever we talk, he refers to several books that he has just read and how those books apply to his business. He always tries to read the top ten business books listed by the Wall Street Journal or the New York Times.

Second, he is not afraid or reluctant to share everything he knows with anyone who is willing to pursue mastery in his or her business. Larry Kendall and Walt Frey have developed a course which contains all the business secrets that Larry has developed. That course is called Ninja Selling® and is the hottest and most relevant selling system in the United States today.

Third, Larry knows his priorities in life and does not deviate from them. His life is ordered by his value system. Last time I checked it was his family first, his business second and his bicycle third. Although Larry is willing to share his knowledge of business, he is not willing to travel all over the United States to do it. So if you want to hear Larry Kendall speak, you will have to go to Colorado!

The Group, Inc., has the distinction of having its real estate agents earn more money and conduct more transactions than any other real estate company in the nation. One of the reasons for that level of success is their business philosophy. When the company started they began to read Mastery by Stewart Emery every day as part of their business plan.

Mastery by Stewart Emery

Mastery in our careers (and in our lives!) requires that we constantly produce results beyond and out of the ordinary. Mastery is a product of consistently going beyond our limits. For most people, it starts with technical excellence in a chosen field and a commitment to that excellence. If you're willing to commit yourself to excellence, to surround yourself with things that represent this excellence, your life will change.

It's remarkable how much mediocrity we live with, surrounding ourselves with daily reminders that average is somehow acceptable. In fact, our world suffers from terminal normality. Take a moment to assess all the things around you that promote your being "average." These are the things that prevent you from going beyond the limits that you've arbitrarily set for yourself.

The first step to mastery is the removal of everything in your environment that represents mediocrity, and one way to attain that objective is to surround yourself with people who ask more of you than you would ordinarily give of yourself. Didn't your parents and some of your best teachers and coaches do exactly that?

Another step on the path to mastery is the removal of resentment toward the masters. Develop compassion for yourself so that you can be in the presence of a master and grow from the experience. Rather than comparing yourself to (and resenting) people who have mastery, remain open and receptive. Let the experience be like the planting of a seed within you that, with nourishment, will grow into your own individual mastery.

You see, we're all ordinary. But rather than condemning himself for his "ordinariness," a master will embrace that ordinariness as a foundation for building the extraordinary. Rather than relying on his ordinariness as an excuse for inactivity, he'll use it instead as a vehicle for correcting himself. It's necessary to be able to correct yourself without invalidating or condemning yourself — to use the results of the correction process to improve upon other aspects of your life. Correction is essential to power and mastery.

Larry Kendall and his agents at The Group, Inc., began reading Stewart Emery's Mastery every day, and it has become central to their philosophy. It has changed the way they think. It has persuaded them to become masters of their business and their lives.

Do you read something each day that will help you become

master of your business and your life? If you did not eat something every day, your body would be hungry. If you do not feed your mind something meaningful every day, it will be hungry as well.

You can become master of your own life, but only if you actively apply yourself to the process. Choose to read Mastery every day for the next twenty-nine days, and it will become a part of your life. You'll begin to see a distinct change in the way you think, act, and react to others.

Plan Your Work, Work Your Plan: The Bear in the Woods

To become a master of your business you have to have a plan. What do you want from your business? When do you want it and how are you going to make it happen?

Uncle Adrian bought Acme Fence Company on the way to work one morning. He had been trying to have some fence installed, but Acme seemed unable to get the work done. He stopped by on his way to work to discuss the delay with the owner. The man said that Acme Fence was swamped with work and could not get to the job any time soon. He also confided in Adrian that he would rather retire and go live at the beach than sell fences. So Uncle Adrian asked him if he would be willing to sell the company, and that's how Adrian was able to buy it.

Uncle Adrian understood how frustrated a customer can feel when he is ready to make a purchase but cannot persuade the business to respond. And Uncle Adrian understood how to respond to a customer's needs.

Uncle Adrian created a simple business plan for his new business. If someone called Acme Fence Company in the morning, the customer would receive a quote on his fence before 5:00pm that afternoon. If he called after lunch, he could count on getting a fencing quote before noon the next day. That modest plan made Acme Fence Company one of the leading fence companies in southeastern North Carolina.

"If you fail to plan, you're planning to fail," Uncle Adrian would say. Unfortunately, the importance of planning becomes obvious only when things go wrong. If you have not planned for your future, you may find yourself in a bad spot someday.

For example, let's consider for a moment a friend of Uncle Adrian's who didn't believe in God. They had conversations about the issue sometimes, but Uncle Adrian was never able to bring his friend around to his way of thinking.

Once, when the friend was out walking in the woods, he was attacked by a bear. Since the bear seemed intent on eating him, out of desperation the man cried, "Lord, save me!"

When nothing happened, the man called out again, "God, I know that I've forsaken You and denounced Your presence. So I realize now that You won't save me — but will You speak to the bear's heart? Will You bestow kindness and gentleness on him and show him Your ways?"

Immediately, the bear rolled off the man, got down on his shaggy knees, folded his front paws together as if in prayer, and began to mumble!

Amazed to see a bear praying and thankful that God had saved him from being eaten, Uncle Adrian's friend decided that he just had to hear what the bear was saying in his prayer. So he crawled over next to the bear and began to listen carefully.

He heard the bear say, "...and Dear Lord, bless this food which I am about to consume."

Most people spend more time planning their vacations than they do planning any other part of their lives. Take the time to plan your business! Take a weekend each year to go to some place that inspires you, away from everyone and everything. Take the time to think about your life and the six areas of mastery. Establish your most important values in life. List all the things you want to accomplish, and plan how you are going to pursue them. What do you want from this year? What do you want from the next five years? What do you want from your life?

Do not wait to establish a plan for your future until you are about to be eaten by a bear!

Customer Service: Saying the Right Thing at the Right Time

My friend Laura just renovated her kitchen, and the building supply store that provided counter tops and cabinets for the job charged her several thousand dollars. When Laura went to the store to pay her bill, she was greeted by a clerk who was too busy to help her. Once the paperwork had been completed the clerk, rather than saying "Thank you for your business," answered her cell phone and walked away. She said and did the wrong thing at the wrong time!

Laura was furious! She felt as if her entire transaction had not been important and she had been taken advantage of. Within the next six months Laura bought two houses and renovated both of them. She used a competing building supply store for all her purchases. The decision to change suppliers was clear. It was all about customer service.

The best part of customer service is saying the right thing at the right time, and Uncle Adrian used to tell a story about a man who always seemed to do exactly that.

Jack woke up with a huge hangover. Forcing himself to open his eyes, he noticed a couple of aspirins beside a glass of water on the night table and next to them, a single red rose. He then saw a note on the table. "Good morning, Honey. Breakfast is on the stove. I'm leaving early to go shopping. Love you!"

Jack sat up, and his clothes were lying at the foot of the bed, all clean and pressed. The bedroom was in perfect order along with the rest of the house. He took the aspirins to dull his headache and then cringed when he saw the huge black eye staring back at him from the bathroom mirror.

He stumbled to the kitchen and sure enough, there was his hot breakfast, with the newspaper. His son was also at the table, eating his morning meal.

Jack asked, "Son, what happened last night?"

"Well, you came home after three in the morning, drunk and out of your mind. You broke some furniture, puked in the hallway, and got that black eye when you ran into the door."

"So why is everything in such perfect order, so clean? I have a rose, and breakfast is on the table, waiting for me!"

His son replied, "Oh, that! Well, Mom dragged you to the bedroom, and when she tried to take your pants off, you screamed, "Leave me alone, lady! I'm a happily married man!"

Saying and doing the right thing, at the right time can solve a lot of problems!

As a customer you should expect and receive customer

service in return for the money you pay a business for its goods and services. However, in today's world, things seem almost the opposite. The employees of some businesses evidently think that the only reason their companies exist is to give them jobs, and the customer is just something that gets in the way.

If your business is losing customers, look no further than the people you have representing you in your store. Examine how they treat the customers who enter your store. Then find a method of teaching your employees to say and do the right thing at the right time.

Presentations:
The Stuttering Bible Salesman

Your ability to present information to others is essential to your success. We present information constantly in an attempt to get others to agree with us or to do the things we need them to do. Everyone makes presentations. Your child makes a presentation when he wants you to buy some candy in the checkout line at the grocery store. Your wife makes a presentation trying to persuade you to take her out to dinner. Your boss makes a presentation trying to get you to work late. Your dog makes a presentation trying to convince you to feed her!

Just think of a seventeen-year-old boy trying to get a date on a Saturday night. He needs to make his presentation to a girl in such a way that she will agree to go out with him. He will take the time to compose exactly what to say to her. He will rehearse his presentation until it's ready, and only then will he proceed with it.

The people who buy from you will base their decisions on the power of your presentation. Your perceived value is based on your ability to communicate information. The way that you present your information makes all the difference in the world.

What if you needed an operation to remove your appendix?

If the surgeon couldn't convince you of this, you might go home from the hospital and die! What about when you bought your house, your car or your health insurance? Do you remember the presentation? What about the fabulously talented artists who created great works of art but died penniless because they didn't know how to present their products to others. Someone has to present all those products or services to the customer in a manner that they can understand so that they will want to buy them.

Let's take a look at your ability to make presentations. How was your last presentation? Did you sell the customer, or did *he* sell *you*? To find an excellent demonstration in the art of presentations, you need look no further than your children. Children understand how to convince others to do what they want. Watch a child if you want to see a great presentation.

First, every child is convinced that whatever they want is the right thing. When a child has made up their mind, there is no hesitation or doubt. They are certain that it's best for him *and* for *you*! It is not possible to do a good job of selling any idea, product, or service that you don't believe in. Sure, you can do it for a while, but if you're going to be a great presenter, you have to believe in what you're selling.

Second, a child will build a list of all the reasons why they should have what they want. If you're going to make a presentation, you will have to have a list of things that support your argument. If one reason will not convince your customer, then another one might.

Third, a child will be relentless in his presentation even if you say no. Saying "no" just adds to a child's pursuit of what he wants because he knows you will say no only about five times. Eventually, you will probably surrender. Uncle Adrian always told me that, when someone says "no," all it really means is that he or she needs more information.

Uncle Adrian was a great presenter. He sold everything from eggs to insurance, and he always said that "in any meeting between two people, one sells, and the other one buys. Either you convince the other fellow to buy something, or he convinces you that he's not going to."

If you needed to learn about making presentations, Uncle Adrian would tell you the story of the stuttering bible salesman.

Southern States Bible Company sold Bibles door to door. Its sales staff mostly consisted of college students working for summer money. One year, during the second week of summer, a new kid showed up at the office.

The young man said, "I...I...I...woo...woo...would like to get a job selling Bi...Bi...Bibles."

The office manager answered, "Wait right here, and I'll check with our sales manager to see if we need any more help."

The office manager went to the sales manager and said, "There's a young man out here who wants a job, but he stutters, and I'm not sure he can sell Bibles door to door. What should I do?"

The sales manager thought for a moment, and then he said, "Give him a case of Bibles, and send him out. If he sells them, great and if he can't sell them, he will have to give them away. Either way we'll be getting Bibles into the hands of more people."

So they gave the young man a case of Bibles to sell and sent him out the door, expecting never to see him again, but at four o'clock that afternoon he returned with every Bible sold! The average salesman needed a week to sell a case of Bibles, yet this stuttering young man had sold all of them in just one day! It was an incredible feat for any salesman, but for someone who stuttered, it was absolutely amazing.

The Sales manager gathered all the salesmen together and said, "Obviously this young man has a great presentation, and all of us can learn from him. Listen closely to his presentation, and tomorrow we want you to do *your* presentation just like *his*!" Then they asked the young man to demonstrate his presentation for everyone in the office.

The young man rose from his seat and walked to the front of the office. Then he stammered, "We...We ...Well, I just go up to the fr...fr...front door of the house and kn...kn...kn...knock on the door. When the lady of the house co...co...comes to the door, I simply say, 'Ma...Ma...Ma'am, I'm here with the So...So...Southern St...St...States Bi...Bi...Bible Company, and I...I...I'd like to se...se...sell you a Bi...Bi....Bible — *or perhaps I should read it to you!*"

Learn how to present information, and you will always have a source of income. Uncle Adrian always said, "Salesmen never get fired. If they can't make a living selling one thing, all they have to do is change products or services and sell something else."

PART SIX

Mastering Your Finances

Uncle Adrian at Price Rite Building Supply

*"Rich people don't work for their money,
their money works for them."*

Uncle Adrian

Wealth Defined:
Feel Rich, Act Rich, and Be Rich

Before you can become master of your life, you must become master of your own finances. Here's Larry Kendall's definition of wealth. "Wealth is the ability to wake up every morning with the time, talent, health, friends, wisdom, passion, and financial freedom to do whatever it is you want to do today."

I used to stop by Acme Fence Company to see Uncle Adrian, and before I would leave, he would always ask, "Boy, have you got money in your pocket?"

I would look into my pocket for my father's old money clip, which I always carried, find a few dollars there, and say, "Sure, Uncle Adrian, I have money in my pocket."

Uncle Adrian would respond, "No, boy — I mean some real money! Here! Take this." He would peel off a hundred-dollar bill from the money he carried in his pocket and say, "Put this in your pocket and carry it around. Don't spend it. Just carry it so you can start to become rich."

I never really understood until much later in life what lesson Uncle Adrian was trying to teach me, but I always took the money, because I usually needed it, and put it in my pocket.

Uncle Adrian would say, "Look, son — if you walk around

broke, you'll feel broke. If you feel broke, you'll act broke. If you act broke, you'll always be broke! But if you have money in your pocket, I mean real money, then every time you put your hand in your pocket, you'll think, 'There's money in my pocket, so I must be rich.'"

"If you have money in your pocket, you'll think you are rich. If you think you're rich, you'll begin to act rich. If you act rich, you'll do the things necessary to become rich. In the end, being rich is just a state of mind."

What's your state of mind when it comes to money? Do you consider yourself wealthy? Do you think like wealthy people think? Wealthy people do not squander their money on lavish living! They put their money to work for them making more money.

How do you start accumulating wealth? You should pay yourself some money to invest out of your next paycheck before you pay any other expenses. You pay the light bill, you pay the phone bill, you make your house payment...but do you pay the most important debt you owe – to yourself and your future investments? Your money is a tool of trade, and you need to act like rich people do by having your money work for you. You need to pay yourself for your future financial security.

Take ten percent of your income from your next paycheck,

and put it into a specially marked account for your future.

Have a little fun! Name your nest egg "My Million-Dollar Account," or whatever will get you emotionally involved in the process. It may be that your employer has a savings plan where you work, or your bank can be instructed to draft ten percent of every one of your checks into a savings program.

Uncle Adrian always said, "I didn't make a lot of money in one place at one time, but I made a little money over a long period of time." How much money will you have in ten years if you do not invest a little of it right now? You have to be disciplined enough to set aside money today, knowing that it is going to work for you in the future.

When I began to accumulate wealth and to see the importance of investing in my future, I finally began to understand what Uncle Adrian had meant when he would ask me, "Boy, have you got money in your pocket?"

Buy Your Own Home:
A Loan for a Frog

The first rule to becoming financially secure is to own your own home. There is no better investment or tax shelter, so home ownership is at an all-time high. Studies show that homeowners become better citizens, voting and taking part in community affairs. Also, they commit fewer crimes and are better educated than other members of society.

Uncle Adrian, Uncle Don, and my father built houses when I was young, and my mother and two of my sisters have built and renovated houses for many years. I have spent most of my adult life involved in the real estate industry as well. You have either bought a house and are paying for it, or you are renting someone else's house and making their payments! Either way, you are paying for a house.

Consider your housing situation for a moment. With the lowest interest rates in the last forty years, your question should be, "What is my dream house, and why am I not living in it?" It is time to own your own home. Get out there, and make it happen.

Now let me show you how you can invest in your mortgage and save thousands of dollars in interest over the life of your loan.

According to the National Association of REALTORS® Research Department, the money that Americans have in the equity value of their homes is greater than the value of all the companies listed on the New York Stock Exchange. You can build equity faster and save thousands of dollars in interest by prepaying the mortgage debt on your home!

You can deduct the mortgage interest from your taxes but you have to pay that money to the mortgage company first. Then you have to wait to get part of it back in taxes a year later! Your home is your best asset in times of need only if it's paid for. If times get tough, you get behind in the payments and the mortgage has not been paid off, the bank will foreclose and take your home.

The mortgage company charges you interest only on the amount of money you owe, calculated on a monthly basis. For instance, a $100,000 mortgage which is amortized at six percent for thirty years has a payment of $600 per month. Over the life of a thirty-year loan, that's 360 payments of $600 each, for a total of $215,838.19. You borrow $100,000 but you pay back $215,838. That is $115,838 in interest! That is more than the cost of the house!

Look closer and you will discover that the first payment of that $100,000 loan is $600, but the interest paid is $500. That is calculated by multiplying the interest rate of six percent times the $100,000 loan amount which equals

$6,000. When you divide $6,000 by twelve monthly payments you get $500 in interest for the first payment. From your $600 payment, $500 goes to interest and only $100 goes toward the actual purchase of your home!

During the second month, your interest is calculated on your current loan balance. If you paid $100 toward your debt of $100,000 in your first payment ($100,000 - $100), then you owe $99,900. For the second payment, the mortgage company multiplies $99,900 by six percent interest, which equals $5994 in interest, then divides that by twelve monthly payments. Your second payment of $600 has $499.50 in interest, and only $100.50 goes toward your loan amount. You paid an additional fifty cents toward the purchase of your home, and you invested six hundred dollars to do it!

If you would like to pay off your mortgage in record time include an additional $100 with your payment. An extra $100 with that first payment would skip payment #2 and go directly to payment #3. You still have to make the payments every month but for every $100 you add you eliminate a payment from the total amount of payments you have to make. The benefit to you is that you would also skip the $500 in interest on payment #2! This is what the mortgage companies don't really want you to know. You can save thousands of dollars in interest over the life of your loan and eliminate lots of payments simply by adding a little extra to your payment every month.

Your savings from making those extra hundred-dollar payments would be huge. First of all, you would save $39,900 in interest on your loan! You would pay off the mortgage in only 270 payments, instead of 360 payments saving $54,000 in payments. If you invested that $54,000 at the same six percent interest rate over the ninety months when you would have been making payments, you would earn $22,000 in interest on your money!

The biggest fear involved in purchasing a home revolves around the mortgage. Just about everyone has to borrow money to buy a home. I have been a REALTOR® for more than twenty years, and I can tell you that, with today's loan programs, most people qualify for a loan.

In fact, I can clearly remember the story Uncle Adrian told me about the frog that got a loan. The frog went into a bank and approached the teller, who, according to her name tag, was Patricia Whack.

The frog said, "Miss Whack, I'd like to get a loan to buy a house."

Patty looked at the frog in disbelief and asked his name.

"My name is Kermit Jagger. My dad is Mick Jagger, and he knows the bank manager."

Patty explained to Kermit that he would need to secure his loan with some collateral. The frog said, "Sure, I have this," and produced a tiny porcelain elephant, about an inch tall and bright pink.

Obviously confused, Patty explained that she would have to consult with the bank manager and disappeared into a back office.

Finding the manager, she said, "There is a frog named Kermit Jagger out there who claims to know you and wants to get a loan. He wants to use this as collateral." She held up the tiny pink elephant and asked, "What in the world is it?"

The bank manager looked back at her and said, "It's a knick-knack, Patty Whack. Give the frog a loan. His old man's a Rolling Stone!"

Getting a loan is easy: any frog can do it. But it takes a pretty smart person to spend an extra hundred dollars a month to save thousands of dollars in interest!

Never Spend Another One-Dollar Bill: The Pickle Jar

For years I always protested that I did not have enough money to invest. Uncle Adrian would say, "Start where you are today!"

The good news is that money does not care how old you are or when you start to invest. Start today with a dollar. Put aside one dollar today to invest, and another one tomorrow. *Never spend another one-dollar bill.*

A good friend of mine, Bryan McKenzie, says that the best way for *him* to save money is never to spend another one-dollar bill. Whenever he breaks a five, ten, or twenty, he simply saves the one's and so far he has saved thousands of dollars — one dollar at a time!

It is amazing how fast they accumulate. The advantage of saving ones is that you cannot rob your savings easily. It's difficult to grab fifty or a hundred dollars in ones and run out to the grocery store or to pay the light bill!

This year my daughter will enter college, so naturally I was discussing the cost with a friend of mine named Bruce and he told me this story about the pickle jar at his house.

As far back as Bruce could remember a pickle jar had sat on

the floor beside the dresser in his parents' bedroom. When his dad got ready for bed, he would empty his pockets and toss his change from the day into the jar.

As a small boy, Bruce had always been fascinated by the sounds the coins made when they were dropped into that pickle jar. If it was almost empty, they landed with a merry jingle; as it came closer to being filled, the tones gradually muted and merged into a dull thud.

Bruce used to squat on the floor in front of the jar and admire the copper and silver circles that glinted like a pirate's treasure when the sun poured through the bedroom window. When the jar was filled with coins that romantic notion gave way to business. Bruce and his dad would sit at the kitchen table and roll the coins before taking them to the bank. Then the coins, which were stacked neatly in a small cardboard box, would be placed between Bruce and his father on the seat of their old truck.

Every time they drove to the bank, Bruce's father would glance at him and say, "These coins are going to send you to college. If we watch our pennies, our dollars will grow." Then at the bank, as he would slide the box of rolled coins across the counter toward the cashier, he would grin proudly and say "These are for my son's college fund."

They would celebrate each deposit by stopping on their way

home for ice cream. Bruce would always get a chocolate and his dad would always get vanilla. When the clerk at the ice cream parlor would hand the father his change, he'd show Bruce the few coins nestled in his palm and say, "When we get home, we will start filling the pickle jar again." He would always let Bruce drop the first coins into the empty jar, and then, as the money rattled around to a cheerful beat, they would grin at each other. "You'll get to college on pennies, nickels, dimes, and quarters if we save a little every day," his father would always say. Eventually those humble coins paid for Bruce's education, and he graduated from college!

Years later, while visiting his parents, Bruce walked into their bedroom to use the phone and noticed that the pickle jar was gone. It had served its purpose and been removed. A lump rose in his throat as he stared at the spot beside the dresser where the jar had always stood. Since his dad was a man of few words, he'd never lectured him on the values of determination, perseverance, and faith. The pickle jar had taught him all these virtues in its own eloquent way. When Bruce married, he told his wife about how significant that jar had been to his childhood. In his mind, the jar defined, more than anything else ever could, how much his dad had loved him.

When Bruce's daughter was born, he and his young family spent the Christmas holiday with his parents. After dinner, his mom and dad sat next to each other on the sofa, taking turns cuddling their first grandchild. When the baby needed changing his wife took the baby into her in-laws' bedroom. When his wife came back into the living room, her eyes were glistening with tears.

Handing her baby back to the brand new grandfather, Bruce's wife took his hand and led him into the bedroom. "Look," she said softly, her eyes directing him to a spot on the floor beside the dresser.

To his amazement, as if it had never been removed, stood the old pickle jar, already holding the beginnings of a new collection of coins. Bruce walked over to the jar, dug down into his pants pocket, and pulled out a handful of coins. With a range of emotions choking him, he dropped in his coins. Then he looked up and saw that his dad had slipped quietly into the room. Their eyes met, and it was obvious that they were sharing identical feelings. Neither father nor son could speak.

Do you have a pickle-jar savings plan? How about a never-spend-a-one-dollar-bill-again savings plan? The key here is to have a *plan to save*. Even if it is only one penny, nickel, dime, quarter or dollar at a time.

PART SEVEN

Becoming Master of Your Own Life

Uncle Adrian at Kings Shopping Center

"Everyone has been given a talent in life. Your job is to find out what your talent is and use it to your fullest potential."

Uncle Adrian

Seven Steps to Mastery:
We Did It This Way Last Year!

Becoming the master of your own life is a process of managing change. By managing the changes that occur in your life, you are always in a state of becoming someone different from who you were yesterday. Every day we grow intellectually and change our lives to match what we think we should be. Most people's lives will be the same tomorrow as they are today because they think the same way day after day. To change your life you have to change the way you think about your future.

There are seven steps to changing anything in your life. First, make the decision to change. Running your life is a chain of conscious decisions, so and you have to consciously decide to make changes in your life. Ask yourself; if I was totally fearless, a hundred times bolder and knew I could not fail, what would I change about my life?

Second, make a list of the reasons you want to change. What or whom do you love enough to make the proposed changes in your life worth the effort. What will your future be like if you don't change?

Third, create a future vision of what your life would be like after the changes. Create written, pictorial and emotional messages about the future you want. Use them to remind yourself of what your life would be like if you made the changes you desire. Play the messages over and over in your mind as many times a day as you can. Take the time to enjoy your future.

Next, transform your visions into important, specific written goals with a deadline for accomplishment. Start with a list of five of the most important accomplishments you would like to make in the next twelve weeks. Evaluate each of these goals. Ask yourself if they are realistic? Are they written out in complete detail? Do you have a realistic deadline for each accomplishment? Are they important to you? What are you willing to give up to accomplish each one?

Fifth, focus on making immediate changes. What are the five most important things you can do tomorrow to begin achieving your twelve week goals? Rate the relative importance of each of tomorrow's goals on a scale of 1 to 5 with one being the most important as it pertains to your future vision of life. First thing tomorrow, begin working on the most important one. Give yourself twenty points for each goal achieved during the day. Play the "Goal Game" each day by allowing your actions to coincide with your goals, which, in turn, are driven by your visions of your future.

Sixth, identify visions, perceptions and actions that will make the changes happen in your life. Write down three patterns of action that you are currently utilizing that will help you achieve your goals. Identify three people in your life that you can ask to help you reach your goals.

Seventh, identify visions, perceptions and actions that may prevent you from making the changes in your life. Write down three patterns of action that you are currently utilizing which may prevent you from achieving your goals. Identify three people in your life that could hold you back from achieving your goals.

Uncle Adrian's story about two friends who refused to change might help you manage changes in your life.

There were two friends named Harold and Mike, and they both lived ridged and unchanging lives. They had been to Kodiak Island, Alaska, for a hunting and fishing trip every year for as long as anybody could remember. Harold loved to say, "We did it this way last year, and we're going to do it the same way this year."

Every year it went just like this: they spent months planning the trip, and when the big day arrived, they went to the airport with all their equipment. The airline employee stated emphatically that they were not getting on board the airplane with their fishing gear and guns. Harold said, "We did it this way last year, and we're going to do it the same way this year!"

Finally, they settled on a solution and were on their way. They reached Alaska after about twenty-four hours of travel, every year. They were exhausted upon arrival, every year.

Harold and Mike made their way to a small harbor on the coast of Alaska to catch a float plane to fly out to Kodiak Island. In the harbor, the wind was howling, and there were whitecaps on the water as the little float plane bounced up and down at the dock. Inside the office, the pilot told them, "We can't fly today. It's too windy. Come back tomorrow!"

Harold said, "We flew out of here last year, and we're going to fly out of here today. We did it this way last year, and we're going to do it the same way this year!" Finally, the pilot agreed, as always, and Harold and Mike loaded their gear onto the airplane to fly to Kodiak Island.

The pilot always landed the plane on a tiny spit of water surrounded by mountains. Harold and Mike's home for the next five days would be a shack built on a short pier that floated on fifty-gallon oil drums. It was the same place every year.

The pilot left the two friends in the wilderness, and for the next five days they hunted, fished and lived off the land, as they did every year. When the plane arrived to take them home again the pilot said, "All this fish, game and equipment will never fit into the plane."

Harold said, "You said the same thing last year but we got it all in the plane. We did it this way last year, and we're going to do it the same way this year!" Finally all the gear was loaded into the plane.

As soon as the pilot cranked up the engine, the pilot said, "The plane is overweight. We may get off the water, but we will never gain enough altitude fast enough to make it over these mountains."

Harold answered, "You said the same thing last year. We did it this way last year, and we're going to do it the same way this year! Now crank up the plane, and let's go home."

After a slow and bumpy take-off, they made a low turn and crashed right into the side of the mountain. The plane skidded to a stop, with fishing gear and guns spread out all over the place. Mike crawled out of the wreckage and yelled, "Harold, where are we?"

Harold shouted back, "I don't know, but it's pretty close to where we crashed last year!"

Are you crashing into the same mountains again and again? Are you making the same mistakes over and over? If so, it's time to make some changes in your life.

Now, become master of your own life and live the life you have always dreamed about!

Zan's Reading List

People often ask me what books I am reading. The following are some of the books that I have found interesting.

Physical Mastery:
Body for Life, Bill Phillips
Dr. Atkins' New Diet Revolution, Robert C. Atkins, MD
Eating for Life, Bill Phillips
Quantum Healing: Exploring the Frontiers of Mind/Body Medicine, Deepak Chopra, MD

Spiritual and Educational Growth:
Conversations with God, Neale Donald Walsch
Eye of the I from Which Nothing Is Hidden,
    David R. Hawkins, MD, PhD
The Field – The Quest for the Secret Force of the Universe,
    Lynne McTaggart
The Road Less Traveled, Scott Peck, MD
Further Along the Road Less Traveled, Scott Peck, MD
How to Know God, Deepak Chopra, MD
Life Applications Study Bible, New Living Translation
The Life You Imagine – Life Lessons for Achieving Your Dreams, Derek Jeter
Objectivism: The Philosophy of Ayn Rand, Leonard Peikoff
Power of Intention: Learning to Co-Create Your World Your Way, Dr. Wayne Dyer

Power vs. Force – The Hidden Determinants of Human Behavior, David R. Hawkins, MD, PhD
Prayer of Jabez, Bruce Wilkinson
7 Habits of Highly Effective People, Stephen R. Covey
Siddhartha, Herman Hesse
The Road Less Traveled, Scott Peck, MD
Tipping Point, Malcolm Gladwell

Relationships:
Anthem, Ayn Rand
Atlas Shrugged, Ayn Rand
Better Way to Live, Og Mandino
Disowned Self, Nathaniel Branden
Honoring the Self, Nathaniel Branden
Inspire! What Great Leaders Do, Lance Secretan
My Personal Best, John Wooden
People of the Lie, Scott Peck, MD
Psychology of Self-Esteem, Nathaniel Branden
The Hidden Messages in Water, Masaru Emoto
Traveler's Gift: Seven Decisions that Determine Personal Success, Andy Andrews
Tuesdays with Morrie, Mitch Albom

Business Mastery:
E Myth, Michael Gerber
E Myth Revisited, Michael Gerber
Greatest Salesman in the World, Og Mandino
Inspirational Leadership, Lance Secretan

Leadership Secrets of Colin Powell, Oren Harari

Lexus and the Olive Tree, Thomas L. Friedman

The Power of Focus, Jack Canfield, Mark Victor Hanson, Les Hewitt

The World is Flat, Thomas L. Freidman

See You at the Top, Zig Zigler

Who Moved My Cheese?, Spencer Johnson

Financial Mastery:

Are You Missing the Real Estate Boom?, David Lereah

If You Want to Be Rich and Happy, Don't Go to School, Robert T. Kiyosaki

Millionaire Next Door, Thomas J. Stanley

Rich Dad, Poor Dad, Robert T. Kiyosaki

Think and Grow Rich, Napoleon Hill

My mission is to inspire and educate
one million people by January 1, 2010.

For additional inspirational material, including
downloadable audio and print library, to purchase
products, or to learn more about Zan Monroe,
visit his website at www.ZanMonroe.com.

Zan Monroe
The Monroe Company, Inc.
PO Box 58241 • Fayetteville NC 28305
1-910-860-4200
Zan@ZanMonroe.com
www.ZanMonroe.com

Zan Monroe

For over thirty years Zan Monroe has been a businessman, speaker, teacher, author, and consultant. More importantly, he's a father, mentor, and friend. He has inspired thousands of people by speaking and teaching across the United States. Inspiring others is what Zan does, whether at home, in business, with friends and family, or speaking to a large audience.

Zan started his first business as a 16-year-old high school student, teaching swimming and tennis in his back yard. He opened Cloverfield Tennis and Swim Club, Inc., his first corporation, at the age of 21. He began his career as a REALTOR® in 1985, working as an agent, sales manager, broker, and owner. He is a member of the National Speakers Association.

Zan lives and works in his hometown of Fayetteville, North Carolina. He has two children, Louisa and Cameron.

Order Form

To order additional copies, fill out this form and send it along with you check or money order to:

The Monroe Company
P.O. Box 58241 • Fayetteville. NC 28305

Cost per copy is $19.95 plus $4.00 P&H
Ship _____ copies of Stories of Uncle Adrian to:

Name: _____

Address: _____

City/State/Zip: _____

_____

☐ check here for signed copy

Please tell us how you found out about this book
☐ Friend   ☐ Radio
☐ Book Store   ☐ Magazine
☐ Newspaper   ☐ Other_____
☐ Internet   _____

Order online at
www.StoriesofUncleAdrian.com